Tom Page
Gisli Thorsteinsson

Technology in Sport

A Debate

LAP LAMBERT Academic Publishing

Impressum/Imprint (nur für Deutschland/ only for Germany)
Bibliografische Information der Deutschen Nationalbibliothek: Die Deutsche Nationalbibliothek verzeichnet diese Publikation in der Deutschen Nationalbibliografie; detaillierte bibliografische Daten sind im Internet über http://dnb.d-nb.de abrufbar.
 Alle in diesem Buch genannten Marken und Produktnamen unterliegen warenzeichen-, marken- oder patentrechtlichem Schutz bzw. sind Warenzeichen oder eingetragene Warenzeichen der jeweiligen Inhaber. Die Wiedergabe von Marken, Produktnamen, Gebrauchsnamen, Handelsnamen, Warenbezeichnungen u.s.w. in diesem Werk berechtigt auch ohne besondere Kennzeichnung nicht zu der Annahme, dass solche Namen im Sinne der Warenzeichen- und Markenschutzgesetzgebung als frei zu betrachten wären und daher von jedermann benutzt werden dürften.

Coverbild: www.ingimage.com

Verlag: LAP LAMBERT Academic Publishing GmbH & Co. KG
Dudweiler Landstr. 99, 66123 Saarbrücken, Deutschland
Telefon +49 681 3720-310, Telefax +49 681 3720-3109
Email: info@lap-publishing.com

Herstellung in Deutschland:
Schaltungsdienst Lange o.H.G., Berlin
Books on Demand GmbH, Norderstedt
Reha GmbH, Saarbrücken
Amazon Distribution GmbH, Leipzig
ISBN: 978-3-8433-7127-8

Imprint (only for USA, GB)
Bibliographic information published by the Deutsche Nationalbibliothek: The Deutsche Nationalbibliothek lists this publication in the Deutsche Nationalbibliografie; detailed bibliographic data are available in the Internet at http://dnb.d-nb.de.
 Any brand names and product names mentioned in this book are subject to trademark, brand or patent protection and are trademarks or registered trademarks of their respective holders. The use of brand names, product names, common names, trade names, product descriptions etc. even without a particular marking in this works is in no way to be construed to mean that such names may be regarded as unrestricted in respect of trademark and brand protection legislation and could thus be used by anyone.

Cover image: www.ingimage.com

Publisher: LAP LAMBERT Academic Publishing GmbH & Co. KG
Dudweiler Landstr. 99, 66123 Saarbrücken, Germany
Phone +49 681 3720-310, Fax +49 681 3720-3109
Email: info@lap-publishing.com

Printed in the U.S.A.
Printed in the U.K. by (see last page)
ISBN: 978-3-8433-7127-8

Tom Page
Gisli Thorsteinsson

Technology in Sport

TECHNOLOGY IN SPORT:

A DEBATE

TOM PAGE & GISLI THORSTEINSSON

THE ABSTRACT

Sport is a very subjective topic; people's opinions will often differ, and therefore encourage debate, frequently resulting in disagreement and argument. Many traditionalists will declare that technology should not be introduced into sport; it should remain how it has been since its creation, played how it was designed to be played. After all, controversies make sport more interesting and ultimately part of what it is today. Others will, however, argue that technology needs to be introduced to aid the official's decisions, to add another interesting dimension, and develop the sport, taking it forward, adapting it to today's modern world. This study, fully analyses whether the introduction of technology into sport is advantageous.

A review of technology already implemented and its implications is discussed, followed by a balanced argument of why technology should and should not be introduced, using case studies, new and old.
Three field sports are contrasted and compared to determine why some sports (and their governing bodies) encourage the use of technology and others do not.

Qualitative research was conducted with three professionals representing each sport in the form of interviews. Opinions are expressed on whether: (1) their sport encourages the use of technology and why; (2) whether the game should be played the same at all levels; (3) the correct decision versus the spectacle for the fans.
Respondents concluded whether or not they thought the introduction of technology in sport was a beneficial step.

From these interviews, accurate information was gained to draw impartial, focussed conclusions.

CONTENTS

Contents

INDEX OF FIGURES

Page Number	Section Number	Section Title	Figure Number	Figure Title	Photo Source

Chapter 1: Introduction

Page Number	Section Number	Section Title	Figure Number	Figure Title	Photo Source
1	1.2	Historical Perspective	Figure 1.2A	Dorando Pietri stumbles over the finish line	Getty Images
2	1.3	The Current Situation	Figure 1.3A	A Historical timeline of a selection of the most famous sporting controversies and technologies introduced	Created by the Author
3	1.3	The Current Situation	Figure 1.3B	Captain Marvel	The Telegraph & BBC Sport

Chapter 2: Review of Literature

Page Number	Section Number	Section Title	Figure Number	Figure Title	Photo Source
4	2.1	Analysis of Existing Literature and Summary of Findings	Figure 2.1A	The Hand of God	Getty Images
4	2.1	Analysis of Existing Literature and Summary of Findings	Figure 2.1B	The Goal that never was	The Guardian
4	2.1	Analysis of Existing Literature and Summary of Findings	Figure 2.1C	The Photo Finish of the Olympic 100m final in 1948	BBC
5	2.1	Analysis of Existing Literature and Summary of Findings	Figure 2.1D	HawkEye analysing a players serve	BBC Sport
6	2.1	Analysis of Existing Literature and Summary of Findings	Figure 2.1E	Hotspot Technology	Cricket Update
6	2.1	Analysis of Existing Literature and Summary of Findings	Figure 2.1F	Signalling the Third Umpire	Getty Images
7	2.1	Analysis of Existing Literature and Summary of Findings	Figure 2.1G	Cricket's Snickometer technology	Channel 4

Chapter 4: Review of Existing Technologies in Place

Page Number	Section Number	Section Title	Figure Number	Figure Title	Photo Source
14	4.2.1	HawkEye	Figure 4.2.1A	The Process HawkEye Undertakes	HawkEye Innovations

15	4.2.1	HawkEye	Figure 4.2.1B	A Historical Timeline of HawkEye's Evolution	Created by the Author
16	4.2.1	HawkEye	Figure 4.2.1C	Top Level of the HawkEye System	Created by the Author
16	4.2.1	HawkEye	Figure 4.2.1D	A shot is called in by HawkEye	HawkEye Innovations
16	4.2.1	HawkEye	Figure 4.2.1E	Glen Mcgrath (bowler) to Left Handers [Batsman]	HawkEye Innovations
17	4.2.2	Umpire Decision Review System	Figure 4.2.2A	The Umpire Decision Review System	The Guardian & Channel 4
17	4.2.2	Umpire Decision Review System	Figure 4.2.2B	The Umpire Review System has received a poor reception	Getty Images
18	4.3	Use of Hotspot	Figure 4.3A	Hotspot gives an indication as to where the ball hit	Mail Online
18	4.5	Television Match Official	Figure 4.5A	The Television Match Official	Static & Getty Images

Chapter 5: Establishing the Need for the Introduction of Technology in Sport

20	5.2	Thierry Henry Case Handball Study	Figure 5.2A	The Hand of Gaul	Sky Sports
21	5.3	David Ngog Dive Case Study	Figure 5.3A	Conning the referee in a blatant manor	Static & 11Gunner
22	5.3	David Ngog Dive Case Study	Figure 5.3B	David Ngog's act of cheating against Birmingham	Mail Online
23	5.4	The Introduction of Two Extra Officials in the Europa League	Figure 5.4A	The Two Extra Assistants	Created by the Author

Chapter 6: Establishing the Need for not Introducing Technology in Sport

26	6.2	FIFA's Point of View	Figure 6.2A	Against changing with the times	BBC & Grab Football
27	6.2	FIFA's Point of View	Figure 6.2B	Grassroots football	Flickr
27	6.3	HawkEye's Tolerance	Figure 6.3A	HawkEye's accuracy has come under fire in recent months	HawkEye Innovations
28	6.4	The 'John McEnroe Factor'	Figure 6.4A	You can not be serious	Getty Images

Chapter 7: Comparing and Contrasting Cricket, Football, & Rugby

30	7.2	The Respective Governing Bodies Opinions	Figure 7.2A	Fédération Internationale de Football Association (FIFA)	Totalfootball
31	7.2	The Respective Governing Bodies Opinions	Figure 7.2B	The Rugby Football Union	RFU
32	7.2	The Respective Governing Bodies Opinions	Figure 7.2C	The England Cricket Board	ECB & Getty Images

Chapter 8: Discussion & Results

35	8.4	Suggestions for Future Research	Figure 8.4A	Fans have strong opinions regarding technology within sport	BBC Sport

INDEX OF TABLES

ACKNOWLEDGEMENTS

SPECIAL THANKS ALSO GOES TO THE INTERVIEWEES, FOR GIVING US A WEALTH OF KNOWLEDGE, WHICH HAS ULTIMATELY MADE THIS STUDY AS SUCCESSFUL AS POSSIBLE.

Chapter 1: Introduction

1.1. Overview of the Topic

Debate is something seen on a daily basis; be it in the form of politics or religion, it is simply something that cannot be escaped. Very rarely is a clear answer in a dispute, an overwhelming accordance with one side, or a lack of passion and that, of course, is what makes it so interesting.

Sport embodies dispute; golfer Phil Mickleson winning events with illegal clubs, sport and controversy seem inseparable. This dissertation explores whether the introduction of technology in sport has beneficial consequences on decision-making and would eliminate controversies, using case studies as further evidence, along with professional opinions where necessary.

1.2. Historical Perspective

Witnessed in the sporting world since the associated sports creation, sporting controversies are nothing new. Ever since the first ball was kicked or first boundary hit, disagreement and controversy was inevitable.

Arguably, the first major sporting controversy was Dorando Pietri's finish in the Olympic marathon in 1908, London.

When Pietri entered the stadium, he went the wrong way and when umpires redirected him, he fell.

He fell four more times, each time the officials helping him up fearing Pietri may die in front of the watching King, Edward VII.

However, completely exhausted, he managed to cross the line first.Rival athletes lodged complaints against the help Pietri received, which were accepted and Pietri was disqualified. This caused huge debate within the athletics community, which still rages on today.

FIGURE 1.2A: DORANDO PIETRI STUMBLES OVER THE FINISH LINE - DURING THE OLYMPIC MARATHON, 1908.

One hundred years ago, there were only a few notable controversies. Today, it seems a football match does not pass without a major talking point (see Figure 1.3A) that could have been solved moments after had technology been used.

1.3. The Current Situation

Sporting controversies have become more common as the years have passed.

Today, the majority of sports players today are professionals, making the stakes far higher than for pre-war sportsmen and women.

1890	*PHOTO FINISH TECHNOLOGY*	[illegible]
1908	*DORANDO PIETRI CONTROVERSY*	THE FIRST RUNNER TO ENTER THE STADIUM DURING THE OLYMPIC MARATHON, DORANDO COLLAPSED METRES FROM THE LINE, HAVING TO BE HELPED ACROSS THE LINE. HE WAS LATER DISQUALIFIED FOR RECEIVING HELP.
1936	*STELLA WALSH'S GENDER*	RUNNING FOR POLAND, WALSH BROKE THREE WORLD RECORDS WHEN COMPETING IN THE 100M. AFTER BEING SHOT TO DEATH IN A ROBBERY IN 1980, THE AUTOPSY SHOWED THAT WALSH WAS IN FACT A MAN.
1950	*INSTANT REPLAY TECHNOLOGY*	[illegible]
1956	*'BLOOD IN THE WATER'*	A WATER POLO MATCH BETWEEN HUNGARY AND THE USSR AT THE MELBOURNE OLYMPICS WAS MADE FAMOUS FOR HUNGARIAN PLAYER ERVIN ZADOR EMERGING FROM THE POOL WITH A GASH UNDER HIS EYE, AND THE RIOT THAT ENSUED.
1964	*BRITISH FOOTBALL BETTING SCANDAL*	EIGHT PROFESSIONAL FOOTBALL PLAYERS WERE JAILED FOR OFFENCES ARISING FROM MATCH FIXING.
1980	*CYCLOPS TECHNOLOGY*	[illegible]
1986	*MARADONA'S 'HAND OF GOD'*	THE 1986 WORLD CUP QUARTER FINAL BETWEEN ARGENTINA AND ENGLAND WAS INFAMOUS FOR MARADONA HANDLING THE BALL INTO THE NET, DUBBED 'THE HAND OF GOD' GOAL, TO CONTRIBUTE TO A 2-1 WIN FOR ARGENTINA.
1999	*SNICKOMETER TECHNOLOGY*	[illegible]
2001	*HAWKEYE TECHNOLOGY*	[illegible]
2002	*BREEDER'S CUP BETTING SCANDAL*	CHRIS HARN CONSPIRED WITH TWO FRIENDS TO MANIPULATE BETS IN THE HORSE RACING BREEDER'S CUP. THIS ENABLED A $3 MILLION PAYOUT TO THE TRIO. THE SCAM WAS EXPOSED WHEN A 43 TO 1 LONGSHOT WON THE CUP.
2004	*HOTSPOT TECHNOLOGY*	[illegible]
2006	*ITALIAN FOOTBALL SCANDAL*	UNCOVERED BY ITALIAN POLICE, JUVENTUS, MILAN, LAZIO, FIORENTINA, AND LAZIO WERE FOUND GUILTY OF RIGGING MATCHES BY SELECTING FAVOURABLE REFEREES.
2007	*MARK CUETO'S DISALLOWED TRY*	ENGLAND PLAYED SOUTH AFRICA IN THE 2007 WORLD CUP RUGBY FINAL. CUETO SCORED WHAT LOOKED TO BE A LEGITIMATE TRY BUT THE TELEVISION MATCH OFFICIAL DISALLOWED IT ON THE BASIS THAT HE COULD NOT FIND A CAMERA ANGLE TO PROVE HIS FOOT HADN'T GONE INTO TOUCH.
2008	*RENAULT'S FORMULA 1 CRASH*	RENAULT ORDERED NELSON PIQUET, JR. TO CRASH INTO A WALL RESULTING IN THE SAFETY CAR BEING DEPOLOYED TO GAIN A SPORTING ADVANTAGE FOR HIS TEAM-MATE FERNANDO ALONSO, WHO WENT ON TO WIN THE RACE.
2009	*THE 'HAND OF GAUL'*	THIERRY HENRY HANDLED THE BALL ILLEGALLY TO SET UP THE WINNING GOAL FOR THE FRENCH AGAINST IRELAND IN THE WORLD CUP PLAY OFF, SENDING FRANCE THROUGH TO THE FINALS AND IRELAND, UNFAIRLY, HOME.
2009	*SERENA WILLIAMS' FOOT FAULT*	WILLIAMS WAS PLAYING KIM CLIJSTERS IN THE SEMI FINAL OF THE US TENNIS OPEN WHEN THE LINE JUDGE DECLARED A FOOT FAULT, A CALL RARELY, IF EVER, SEEN AT THAT STAGE OF A MATCH (MATCH POINT).
2010	*CRICKET BALL TAMPERING*	PAKISTAN CRICKETER SHAHID AFRIDI WAS CITED BITING THE BALL DURING A TEST MATCH AGAINST AUSTRIALIA TO ENCOURAGE THE BALLS SWING/REVERSE SWING THROUGH THE AIR, DECEIVING BATSMAN ILLEGALLY.

FIGURE 1.3A: A HISTORICAL TIMELINE OF A SELECTION OF THE MOST FAMOUS SPORTING CONTROVERSIES AND TECHNOLOGIES INTRODUCED (GREY BOXES).

Previously, people were driven by the enjoyment of taking part, which often led to the sportsperson enjoying the competition, and, win or lose, shaking their oppositions hand come the end.

Nowadays however, there is far more pressure involved in professional sport.

Far more than simple enjoyment occupies the world stage of sport – times have changed; opinions and attitudes have altered. The sportsman's career could hinge on one single decision the referee makes in a high profile match.

The media have had a huge role to play in the dynamics of sport, and will continue to do so.

Nowadays the media brand a club 'in crisis' if they go a few games without a win.

Modern media over emphasise situations, piling the pressure on teams and players, needlessly.

In the run up to the 2007 Rugby World Cup, the English media were billing England as 'out of sorts' and in 'appalling form', which could only have dented the players' confidence.

It seems the media make efforts to load pressure on sports people, despite the achievement of their national team being at stake.

The mentality of today's player has evolved through the pressure of media. Feeling the need to perform well in every game and the importance of winning come what may, is why controversies are seen more commonly – opinions will always contrast.

Figure 1.3b: Captain Marvel - John Terry is often regarded as one of Chelsea's finest captains due to his passion.

As the stakes increase, as media pressure amplifies, as more money is involved, and careers depend upon decisions, there will be more argument involved, and more controversy.

Most governing bodies do not want their sport tarnished by disagreement, and therefore encourage the development of technology (see *Chapter 4*).

1.4. THE ARGUMENTS THAT EXPLAIN THE RATIONALE FOR THE STUDY

There has not been a paper, or book that analyses sporting controversies and the influence the introduction of technology has upon sport, although there are many papers that research some aspects of this topic.

There is nothing that currently brings all of this together into one significant study.

Sports governing bodies often talk about the introduction of certain technologies and the reasons for and against the introduction.

This dissertation gives an impartial investigation into the use of technology in sport, from every perspective possible – the players, authorities, technology creators, to arrive at a conclusion based on appropriate research.

CHAPTER 2: REVIEW OF LITERATURE

2.1. ANALYSIS OF EXISTING LITERATURE AND SUMMARY OF FINDINGS

Many sources of relevant information have been consulted to gain an understanding of existing literature about the use of technology in sport. These have predominantly come in the form of online journals; however, these have been supported by books and websites.

FIGURE 2.1A: THE HAND OF GOD - DIEGO MARADONA ILLEGALLY HANDLES THE BALL TO GUIDE IT OVER PETER SHILTON IN 1986.

FIGURE 2.1B: THE GOAL THAT NEVER WAS - FREDDIE SEARS SCORES A GOAL AGAINST BRISTOL CITY THAT HITS THE BACK OF THE NET AND BOUNCES OUT AFTER STRIKING THE STANCHION; THE GOAL WAS NOT GIVEN.

Controversy has surrounded the sport for many years – the two seem inseparable. From Maradona's infamous 'Hand of God' incident in the Mexico 1986 FIFA World Cup, (Figure 2.1A) to Freddie Sears' goal for Crystal Palace F.C., that was never given (Figure 2.1B) –controversial decisions are nothing new.

These controversies have always occurred but Holmes (2007) argues that they are part of what makes sport so interesting, creating discussion and argument.

Perhaps this is why football drags its heels and refuses to embrace technology available to assist referees. Yet, other sports such as rugby, cricket, and tennis have been able to effectively accommodate the use of technology to ensure that officials make the correct decision.

FIGURE 2.1C: THE PHOTO FINISH OF THE OLYMPIC 100M FINAL IN 1948.

Discussed in *1.3: The Current Situation,* controversies are becoming increasingly common, as the financial stakes and media pressures rise within professional sport. Technology will prevent some future controversies, but there are many conflicting arguments about the introduction of technology, cited below.

The first real technology introduced in the sporting world was the photo finish. Developed in 1899, the photo finish produces a series of still photo frames, determining positions at real time speeds that the human eye cannot distinguish.

Greenberg (2005) recognises that before 1948 there was no automatic timing in use – the photo finish was only used to aid the judges to decide placings.

Automatic timing systems were introduced in 1952. Greenberg goes on to say that the difference between the automatic timings and 'official' manual timings was excessive, making previous timings invalid, inevitably leading to controversy regarding records.

The 'Cyclops' technology used in tennis from 1980 until 2007 was another one of the earliest technologies to enter the sporting world. However, "it came with many problems; it was limited to the service line, prone to error, and because it relied on beams on infrared light, Cyclops could be set off by insects or other stray objects". (Pilhofer, A. 2008).

HawkEye Innovations unveiled 'HawkEye' in 1999.
The response to this technology was fascination and excitement, something vastly superseding the benchmark 'Cyclops' technology in terms of accuracy and depth.

Pilhofer (2008) published the online article 'A Replay System that is a Hit among Players, Fans and Even Officials' in 2008. This article included an interview with the inventor of HawkEye –Paul Hawkins.
"During warm days, the court actually changes size as it heats up or cools down. When the ball flight data is fed into the computer model, the result is a system that is so precise it's difficult to measure." (Hawkins, P. 2008).
Hawkins stressed the degree of accuracy of the tool, which has recently come under scrutiny.
Pilhofer concluded that the data HawkEye is able to capture and process in a user-friendly form is invaluable in helping viewers gain a unique insight into how the best players in the world are able to achieve all they do.

Inevitably, however, HawkEye has some critics amongst players and the media.

Collins and Evans (2008) carried out a study at Cardiff University regarding the accuracy of HawkEye in Tennis, disputing HawkEye Innovations' stated precision.
"Rafael Nadal hit a ball which appeared to viewers, the umpire, and to Federer as impacting well behind the baseline, but HawkEye called it in." (Collins, H. and Evans, R. 2008. p. 1).

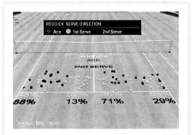

FIGURE 2.1D: HAWKEYE ANALYSING A PLAYER'S SERVES - THE CARDIFF UNIVERSITY STUDY (2008) COMPLETELY NEW DIMENSION TO ANALYSING TENNIS IT SHOULD NOT BE USED AS A FIRST HAND DECISION MAKING TOOL ON COURT.

The article went on to state that although Nadal's forehand was called in by 1mm, HawkEye Innovations report that the average error of the machine is 3.6mm. If the Cardiff analysis is correct, the errors can be even larger than 3.6mm on some occasions.
"The International Tennis Federation, which tests the machines for use, accept HawkEye had passed its test if it called the ball in by 1mm while the true position was out by 5mm." (Collins, H. and Evans, R. 2008. p. 1).
The research team at Cardiff University, led by Professor Collins and Doctor Evans, stated technologies such as HawkEye have been designed to eliminate line call controversies, however, their analysis showed that Hawkeye is not always correct and therefore should not be relied on as the definitive decision maker.
"The analysis also concludes that HawkEye might be in danger of unnecessarily changing the traditional nature of certain games because it does not take account of traditional areas of systematic error when making judgements." (Collins, H. and Evans, R. 2008. p. 2).
The study concluded that while HawkEye is an interesting tool that brings a whole new dimension to viewing the game for commentators, analysts, and household viewers it should be left at that, and not be used as a definitive decision making tool on court, until vastly improved.

Test Cricket has recently implemented the 'Review System'. This gives each team three reviews per innings, providing the chance to check the umpire's decision with the third umpire. The third umpire has HawkEye at their disposal, assisting them in reaching the correct decision.

In his article 'Technology in Sport – Cricket Referral System', Renshaw (2007) believes that the system is designed to reduce only the major errors, so with only three challenges per side it is used sparingly and only when players genuinely believe they have a chance of overturning incorrect decisions.
However, Renshaw does state that the one of the criticisms levelled against it is that it erodes the integrity and authority of the umpires.

Yet, Mac (2007) disagrees, stating that Renshaw's argument does not carry much weight, as some decisions are unclear to the umpires on the field. When this happens, the decision is sometimes reviewed by the third umpire, who then uses HawkEye to arrive at the correct decision. Players being able to challenge decisions will just be an extension of this.

Hotspot is another technology used by television analysts, but more importantly, not often obtainable to the third umpire when investigating decisions.

Ting and Chilukuri (2009) explain: "Hotspot is an infrared imaging system used to determine whether the ball strikes the batsman, bat or pad. The technology works by placing infrared cameras at either end of the pitch. These cameras identify the heat generated from the ball hitting the batsman's (Figure 2.1E) bat or pad. A negative image is then produced using a computer which shows the exact point of contact between the ball and the batsman."

FIGURE 2.1E: HOTSPOT TECHNOLOGY - THE HOTSPOT, SEEN AT THE TOP OF THE BATSMAN'S RIGHT LEG PAD, INDICATES THE BATSMAN WAS TRAPPED LBW.

Although Hotspot has been welcomed warmly since its introduction in 2006, Dorries (2009) suggests there is not much point in making this technology available to the third umpire.
Dorries' article 'Cricket Referral System under Fire' uses a case study to advocate this suggestion further.
"Ian Gould raised his finger when Aussie Mitchell Johnson had appeared to dab a spinning delivery to the wicketkeeper.
Johnson challenged the decision and several video replays were unclear – although they did appear to show that Johnson had hit his own pad rather than the ball.
Then Channel's Nine's Hotspot technology was summoned and revealed no clear evidence that the ball had glanced Johnson's bat – in fact, it almost certainly had not. So should the benefit of the doubt go to Johnson?"
Johnson was actually given out. Gould got the benefit of the doubt with his original decision. It was a confusing state of affairs because Johnson probably was not out.

FIGURE 2.1F: SIGNALLING THE THIRD UMPIRE - UMPIRE IN THE MIDDLE, IAN GOULD ASKS THE THIRD UMPIRE AFTER MITCHELL JOHNSON (BATSMAN) ASKED FOR HIS DISMISSAL TO BE REFERRED DURING DAY TWO OF AUSTRALIA VS. THE WEST INDIES, 2009.

Dorries goes on to describe this example as "another intriguing chapter in cricket's man-versus-machine debate" and if nothing else it has proved that umpires have some doubts about the technology.

Dorries also identifies that there is no point in using Hotspot when third umpires are not going to trust it, or if it is not conclusive.

He concludes: "Maybe Hotspot should just remain with analysts and for us at home to enjoy, and not plague the third umpires mind with doubts and indecision." This view resembles Cardiff University's that HawkEye should not be a first hand decision-making tool.

Mitchell (2009) briefly touches on Hotspot and its limitations in his *article 'In the Blink of a HawkEye, Cricket has changed forever'* - "Another problem is the length of time it takes to make decisions."

Mitchell also cited the Gould/Mitchell incident as an example. "Everyone at the Gabba [sports stadium, Brisbane] could have gone to the toilet, bought a pie and a beer and then returned to their seats before Johnson learned of his fate."

Mitchell concludes that it is a clever tool, and there is no doubt it is interesting, but if the third umpire cannot decide on Leg before Wicket (LBW) incidents with it, there is no point providing him with this technology.

THE BALL TRAVELS TOWARD THE BAT EDGE.

THE BALL CLIPS THE BAT EDGE, RESULTING IN THE SOUND LINE MAGNIFYING, INDICATING THIS.

FIGURE 2.1G: CRICKET'S SNICKOMETER TECHNOLOGY.

The final commonly used technology to be seen in televised cricket is 'Snickometer'.

Bull (2009) explains: "Essentially it is a highly sensitive microphone that is placed in the batsmans' off stump and connected to an oscilloscope that measures the sound waves of an oncoming ball. When the ball nicks the bat, the oscilloscope trace goes wild, and by analysing the video stream in extreme slow motion alongside this graph, you can see whether of not the noise picked up by the microphone coincides with the ball passing the bat."

Ting and Chilukuri (2009) state in their paper *'Novel Pattern Recognition Technique for an Intelligent Cricket Decision Making System'* that "it is often one of the most difficult tasks for an umpire: deciding whether a ball has clipped the bat or part of the player's protective equipment on its way to the wicketkeeper."

However, Snickometer is not available to the third umpire when reviewing decisions, only to television coverage.

While commentating on the 2009 Ashes series [between England and Australia], ex-England cricket captain Nasser Hussain stated that this technology should be made available to the third umpire.

"The Snickometer is handy at resolving issues, yet it is not obtainable to third umpires? This surely has to be stupidity, umpires not giving a batsman out when a commentary team a matter of metres away from the third umpire can see they clearly should be with the use of Snickometer."

Thaindian News (2008) released an article *'Third Umpire checks with Broadcaster's Snickometer'* to demonstrate the benefit of providing this technology to the third umpire: "A controversy over Mike Hussey's dismissal, given out by the third umpire. Hussey clearly hit the ball and umpire Taufel referred the decision to see whether it had carried to the wicketkeeper.

The ball clearly carried but the third umpire strangely checked Channel Nine's Snickometer to confirm the edge."

The correct decision was reached with, what Hussain calls, "a logical method of giving the third umpire all the technology possible".

However, in their paper 'The HawkEye Technology', Gangal & Raje (2009) disagree and argue that the Snickometer should be left for television companies to interest viewers and not for the third umpire's use.
They cite that it is too inconclusive to hinge what may be a match changing decision on the tool by itself.

It can be concluded that there a many conflicting opinions regarding technology in sport, discussed by commentators, professionals, and members of the public alike, but will always spark disagreement and debate.

2.2. Formulation of Key Questions

With the literature review completed, sources have addressed many relevant issues already. However, some topics remained unanswered, which were addressed in the body of this study. These points have been summarised into key questions.

1) How has the introduction of technology in decision-making/supporting technology to date changed sport?

2) What are the key reasons for introducing decision-making/supporting technology into sport?

3) What are the key reasons for not introducing decision-making/supporting technology into sport?

4) Why do some sports encourage the use of decision-making/supporting technology but others do not?

5) Why do some associations not want the introduction of decision-making/supporting technology?

CHAPTER 3: METHODS & ISSUES

3.1. INTRODUCTION

Many research types were analysed to determine what methods would be best suited for gathering research to form reliable conclusions from.
The method of research used to collect this primary research was established – discussed in *Section 3.3*.

3.2. SUMMARY OF SPECIFIC RESEARCH UNDERTAKEN FOR EACH KEY QUESTION

	Key Question	Chapter the Question is Answered within	Research Undertaken
1	How has the introduction of technology in decision-making/supporting technology to date changed sport?	Chapter 4: Review of Existing Technologies in Place	Literature Review/Analysing various sources - journals, books, webpages
2	What are the key reasons for introducing decision-making/supporting technology into sport?	Chapter 5: Establishing the Need for the Introduction of Technology in Sport	Case studies analysed ably backed up with supporting evidence from journals and webpages
3	What are the key reasons for not introducing decision-making/supporting technology into sport?	Chapter 6: Establishing the Need for not Introducing Technology in Sport	Carried out in the same manor as question 2, many sources of secondary research were looked into
4	Why do some sports encourage the use of decision-making/supporting technology but others do not?	Chapters 5, 6 & 8	As well as looking at previous statements released by governing bodies, interviews were conducted with professionals
5	Why do some associations not want the introduction of decision-making/supporting technology?	Chapters 5, 6 & 8	From these interviews this key question has been answered, but was also supported with secondary research, such as information from websites etc

TABLE 3.2A: A SUMMARY OF THE KEY QUESTIONS AND IN WHICH CHAPTERS THEY HAVE BEEN ADDRESSED.

3.3. ANALYSING POTENTIAL RESEARCH TYPES

3.3.1. QUANTITATIVE RESEARCH

"Quantitative research is a means for testing objective theories by examining the relationship among variables. These variables, in turn, can be measured, typically on instruments, so that numbered data can be analysed using statistical procedures." (Creswell, J. W. 2009).

Quantitative research is used to measure how many people think or act in a particular way using figures and numbers.

Although quantitative research may seem favourable due to the fact it can be used to sample a large scale to ensure answers are statistically correct, there are some clear disadvantages.

Nykiel (2007) cites the following reasons why quantitative research is disadvantaged compared to qualitative research:

- Quantitative research collects a narrower, sometimes superficial, dataset. Results are limited as they provide numerical descriptions rather than detailed descriptions.

- The research is undertaken in an unnatural, artificial environment so that a level of control can be applied to the exercise.

- The development of standard, structured questions can lead to bias and false representation.

The period allocated to carry out and complete the study made the feasibility of gathering participants and testing unrealistic. Opinionated, not numerical, responses were needed; and it is for these reasons that quantitative research was not used when researching.

3.3.2. MIXED METHOD RESEARCH

"Mixed methods research is an approach that combines both qualitative and quantitative forms. It involves philosophical assumptions, the use of qualitative and quantitative approaches, and the mixing of both approaches." (Creswell, J. W. 2009).

Mixed methods use factors from both qualitative and quantitative approaches, such as pre-determined (quantitative) and emerging methods (qualitative).

Therefore, mixed method research is the most effective way to reach a conclusion, drawing upon statistical and text analysis.

Quantitative Methods	Mixed Methods	Qualitative Methods
• Pre-determined • Instrument based questions • Performance data, attitude data, observational data, and census data • Statistical analysis • Statistical interpretation	• Both pre-determined and emerging methods • Both open- and closed-ended questions • Multiple forms of data drawing on all possibilities • Statistical and text analysis • Across databases interpretation	• Emerging methods • Open-ended questions • Interview data, observation data, document data, and audio-visual data • Text and image analysis • Themes, patterns interpretation

TABLE 3.3.2A: QUANTITATIVE, MIXED, AND QUALITATIVE METHODS. SOURCE: CRESWELL, J. W. (2009) "RESEARCH DESIGN", (ED. 3), PP.15, LONDON: SAGE PUBLICATIONS, INC.

However, it relies on quantitative research.

The research will not need a numerical input to gain an informative conclusion.

Hence, quantitative and mixed method research was not used when carrying out research.

3.3.3 QUALITATIVE RESEARCH

"Qualitative research is a means for exploring and understanding the meaning individuals or groups ascribe to a social or human problem. The process of research involves emerging questions and procedures, data typically collected in the participant's setting." (Adapted from Creswell, J. W. 2009).

Qualitative research is all about exploring issues, understanding phenomena and answering questions.
This type of research aids the understanding about how people feel and why they feel the way they do. It is concerned with collecting in-depth information with subjects. The sample size tends to be smaller than quantitative projects.

Two of the most common types of qualitative research are:

- Case Studies

Case studies are an in depth study of a particular situation rather than a sweeping statistical survey. They are usually performed to narrow down a very broad field of research into one easily researchable topic.
Case studies have been used in chapters five and six to narrow down broader arguments.

- Interviews

There are many types of interviews; however, the most appropriate for the conclusions desired is semi structured open-ended interview: "understanding the world from the subjects' point of view." (Kvale, S. 1996).

"Researchers using this approach prepare a set of open-ended questions which are carefully worded and arranged for the purpose of minimising variation in the questions posed to the interviewees." (Sewell, M. 2005).

3.4. INTERVIEWS

Sewell (2005) identifies the following advantages of conducting qualitative based semi structured open-ended interviews:

- They allow the participant to describe what is meaningful to them using their own words rather than being restricted to predetermined categories; resulting in participants feeling more relaxed and honest.

- They provide high credibility.

- Allows the researcher to probe for more details and ensure that participants are interpreting questions correctly.

- Interviewers have the flexibility to use their knowledge, expertise, and interpersonal skills to explore unexpected ideas.

Thus, semi structured, open-ended interviews have many relevant advantages that will provide the correct type of answers to reveal conclusions.

3.5. SUBJECT SELECTION & QUALITY

Interviews will be conducted with a small group of professionals to gain first hand opinions about whether the introduction of technology in sport is beneficial or not. *Chapter 7: The Comparison of Cricket, Football & Rugby* looks into the respective opinions of governing bodies regarding technology.
It seems logical to interview representatives from those sports, to continue comparing and contrasting between the sports.

Sewell (2005) states that the researcher has to minimise the variation in the questions posed. The questions posed to each representative must remain as similar as possible.

After contact was initiated, three interviews were organised with a representative from each sport:

- Michael Bourne from the England Cricket Board (ECB) – England Cricket's *Head of Performance Analysis*.

- Christopher Walsh from the Suffolk Football Association (FA) – *Suffolk Football Development Officer*.

- A delegate from the Rugby Football Union (RFU) – happy to give opinions but wished to remain unnamed.

These representatives were selected because it was advised from each organisation that they would be able to offer the most factual and in depth answers.

3.6. CONCLUSIONS

Qualitative research is implemented throughout this study.

Cases studies in chapters five and six offer in depth analysis of occasions to demonstrate certain opinions.

After comprehensively analysing all the potential research types (Table 3.6A), it was established that open-ended interviews would be used to gather professionals opinions on the subject.

These professionals were contacted and interviews organised.
However, many factors have to be considered before carrying out these discussions.

"Reliability is the degree to which a test is consistently measured". (Creswell, J. W. 2009).

Miles and Huberman (1994) state that to make a study reliable, recording methodology when gathering data has done carefully.
Prior to any interview being conducted, potential bias was examined.
The interviewer may subconsciously give subtle clues in body language, or tone of voice, that subtly influence the subject into giving answers skewed towards the interviewer's own opinions, prejudices and values.

This is carefully avoided when conducting interviews with professionals.

To eliminate the risk of any bias the interviewer was completely objective and remained neutral throughout the study.

Category	Research	What is it?	Supporting Quotes	Positives	Negatives
Quantitative Research	Survey Research	Provides a quantitative or numeric description of trends, attitudes, or opinions of a population by studying a sample using questionnaires or structured interviews	"Determine the relationship between one thing [independent variable] and another [dependant] in a population." (Hopkins, W. G. 2002).	Provides a statistical conclusion	Generalises and assumes the taken sample is representative of the whole population
				—	Does not give the interviewee a chance to express their opinions as fully as they may like
	Experimental Research	Seeks to determine if a specific treatment influences an outcome. The impact is assessed by providing a specific treatment to one group and not the other, the determining how many groups scored on an outcome	"Experiments include true experiments, with the random assignment of subjects to treatment conditions, and experiments that use nonrandomised designs." (Keppd, G. 1991).	Provides a conclusion to which treatments are successful	The groups selected assumes they will be a representation of the whole population
Mixed Methods	Sequential Mixed	A procedure where the research seeks to elaborate on or expand on the findings of one method with another	"This may begin with a qualitative interview for exploratory purposes and follow up with a quantitative survey with a large sample so the researcher can generalise results to a population." (Creswell, J. W. 2009).	Provides statistical and text analysis	—
				Can give the interviewees the opportunity to expand upon answers	
				Multiple forms of data drawing on all possibilities	
	Concurrent Mixed	A multi-strand design in which both qualitative and quantitative date are data and analysed to answer a single type of research question	"Converges or merges quantitative and qualitative data in order to provide a comprehensive analysis of the research problem." (Creswell, J. W. 2009).	Can analyse different types of questions more easily	—
				Collect both forms of data at the same time and then integrates the information all together	
Qualitative Research	Ethnography	A strategy of inquiry in which the researcher studies an intact cultural group in a natural setting over a prolonged period of time by collecting observational and interview data	—	Flexible and typically evolves contextually in response to the lived realities encountered in the field setting	Conducted over a long period of time
				Provides an accurate conclusion	
	Case Studies	A strategy in which the researcher explores in depth a program, event, activity, process, of one of more individuals	"Case studies are bounded by time and activity, and researchers collect detail information using a variety of data collection procedures over a sustained period of time." (Stake, R. E. 1995).	Can be effective at proving certain points of view	Narrow down a broader field, but can sometimes an unrealistic representation
	Interviews (Semi Structured)	Interviews consist of a set prepared of open-ended questions which are carefully worded and arranged for the purpose of minimising variation in the questions posed to the interviewees	"used to understand the world from the subjects' point of view, to unfold the meaning of peoples' experiences, to uncover their lived world prior to scientific explanations." (Kvale, S. 1996).	Lets the interviewee express their true opinions, allowing elaboration	—
				Provide high credibility	
				Allows the potential for the interviewer to probe for more details	

TABLE 3.6A: A SUMMARY OF THE TYPES OF RESEARCH AVAILABLE TO USE - CASE STUDIES HAVE BEEN USED, FOLLOWED BY INTERVIEWS WITH A SERIES OF PROFESSIONALS.

CHAPTER 4: REVIEW OF EXISTING TECHNOLOGIES IN PLACE

4.1. INTRODUCTION

It was important to establish how existing technologies already seen in the world of sport have been embraced, how they have affected opinions and attitudes, and most importantly, to what degree the introduction has changed sport.

Analysing these factors have answered the first key question: *How has the introduction of technology in decision-making/supporting technology to date changed sport?*

4.2. USE OF HAWKEYE & REVIEW SYSTEM

4.2.1. HAWKEYE

HawkEye is a computer system used primarily in cricket and tennis, but also in snooker, to visually track the path of the ball and display a record of its most statistically likely path as a moving image.

Developed in 1999, and first used in 2002, HawkEye entered the sporting world as arguably the most sophisticated officiating tool, offering a unique blend of innovation, experience and accuracy.

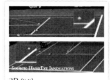   

2D (x,y)	3D (x,y,z)	4D (x,y,z,t)	
THE POSITION OF THE BALL IN TERMS OF BOTH THE DEPTH AND SIDEWAYS MOVEMENT ON THE COURT IS CALCULATED FROM EACH FRAME.	STRATEGICALLY PLACED CAMERAS ALSO CAPTURE THE HEIGHT OF THE BALL FROM THE PLAYING SURFACE, CAMERA MOVEMENT IS COMPENSATED FOR BY TRACKING THE LINES OF THE COURT.	THIS PROCESS IS REPEATED FOR EACH FRAME SO THAT THE 3D POSITIONS OF THE BALL CAN BE COMBINED TO PRODUCE A SINGLE TRAJECTORY OF THE FLIGHT OF THE BALL.	THE TRAJECTORY IS THEN USED TO CALCULATE WHERE THE BALL WILL LAND ON THE COURT. ACCORDING TO THE RULES OF THE GAME THE CALL IS THEN MADE.

FIGURE 4.2.1A: THE PROCESS HAWKEYE UNDERTAKES - CAMERAS TRACK THE BALL AT A RATE OF 60 TIMES A SECOND.

Cameras installed at six to ten positions around the court monitor the court and send video into four mainframes, which then combine all the information. Machine vision software combines the references to determine the ball's three-dimensional position. Computers process frame positions through time to track the ball's trajectory and determine where it contacts the court.

For years, umpires have looked for ball marks to help decide close line-calls; now HawkEye can calculate actual compression.

1999	RESEARCH BEGINS	RESEARCH BEGINS AT ROKE MANOR RESEARCH LTD., A COMPANY WITH OVER THIRTY YEARS OF VISION PROCESSING EXPERTISE - HAWKEYE IS BORN.
2001	INTRODUCED IN THE ASHES	AFTER EIGHTEEN MONTHS OF DEVELOPMENT, CHANNEL 4 USE HAWKEYE IN THEIR COVERAGE OF THE ASHES, WINNING A BAFTA FOR 'SPORTS INNOVATION' IN THE PROCESS.
2001 SEPTEMBER	DEVELOPED FOR TENNIS	HAWKEYE INNOVATIONS LTD. IS LAUNCHED AS A SEPARATE COMPANY. THE TENNIS SYSTEM RECEIVES A NEW IMPETUS OF DEVELOPMENT EXPERTISE.
2002 FEBRUARY	INTRODUCED IN TO TENNIS	HAWKEYE IS FIRST USED IN TENNIS AS PART OF THE BBC'S DAVIS CUP COVERAGE.
2003 JANUARY	TENNIS GRAND SLAM DEBUT	HAWKEYE MAKES ITS GRAND SLAM TELEVISION DEBUT AT THE AUSTRALIAN OPEN.
2004 SEPTEMBER	UMPIRING CONTROVERSY	JENNIFER CAPRIATI'S 2-6, 6-4, 6-4 QUARTERFINAL VICTORY OVER SERENA WILLIAMS AT THE U.S. OPEN THRUSTS LINE-CALLING INTO THE MEDIA SPOTLIGHT. THE USTA ACKNOWLEDGED THAT CHAIR UMPIRE OVERRULE AGAINST WILLIAMS IN THE FIRST GAME OF THE FINAL SET WAS INCORRECT.
2005 OCTOBER	ACCURACY TEST PASSED	HAWKEYE PASSES STRINGENT ITF TESTS; CORRECTLY CALLING MORE THAN EIGHTY BALLS FIRED ON COURT IN NEW YORK.
2005 DECEMBER	OFFICIAL REVIEW DEBUT	THE HAWKEYE OFFICIAL REVIEW SYSTEM MAKES IT DEBUT IN THE CHAMPIONS TOUR AT THE ROYAL ALBERT HALL.
2006 SUMMER	USED AT THE US OPEN SERIES	OFFICIALLY USED AT THE 10 U.S. OPEN SERIES EVENTS AND THE WORLD TEAM TENNIS TOUR THROUGHOUT AMERICA.
2007 JANUARY	ENGLISH FOOTBALL CONTRACT	HAWKEYE AGREES A CONTRACT WITH THE ENGLISH PREMIER LEAGUE TO DEVELOP GOAL-LINE TECHNOLOGY FOR FOOTBALL.
2007 JANUARY	CHALLENGE SYSTEM DEBUT	NEW VIDEO BOARDS DISPLAYING HAWKEYE DEBUT AT THE AUSTRALIAN OPEN. PLAYERS ARE ALLOWED TWO INCORRECT CHALLENGES PER SET, WITH THE BENEFIT OF AN ADDITIONAL CHALLENGE IF THE SET GOES TO A TIE-BREAK.
2007 FEBRUARY	IFAB APPROVAL	THE INTERNATIONAL FOOTBALL ASSOCATION BOARD (IFAB) GIVES ITS APPROVAL FOR HAWKEYES FOOTBALL DEVELOPMENT WORK.
2007 JUNE	INTRODUCTION TO WIMBLEDON	HAWKEYE IS USED OFFICIALLY AT THE WIMBLEDON CHAMPIONSHIPS, THE THIRD GRAND SLAM EVENT TO IMPLEMENT THE TECHNHOLOGY.
2007 AUGUST	GOAL-LINE TECHNOLOGY	HAWKEYES FOOTBALL GOAL-LINE TECHNOLOGY PASSES THE FIRST STAGE OF TESTING BY THE FA PREMIER LEAGUE.
2007 SEPTEMBER	WORLD TWENTY 20 DEBUT	HAWKEYE SENDS THREE UNITS TO THE INAUGURAL ICC WORLD TWENTY20 CHAMPIONSHIPS IN SOUTH AFRICA.
2007 OCTOBER	DEVELOPING PLAYER CHALLENGE	THE MCC WORLD CRICKET COMMITTEE ANNOUNCE THAT HAWKEYE WILL BE USED IN TRIALS TO DETERMINE A NEW PLAYER CHALLENGE SYSTEM IN TEST CRICKET.
2008 AUGUST	PULSE DEBUT	HAWKEYES BROTHER COMPANY, PULSE, MAKES ITS DEBUT AT THE U.S. OPEN. PULSE GIVES FANS THE OPPORTUNITY TO EXPRESS THEIR OPINION, TRACK PLAYER AND TOURNAMENT PROGRESS, IMPROVE THEIR TENNIS KNOWLEDGE, AND PREDICT THE GAME-BY-GAME OUTCOME OF THE MATCH

FIGURE 4.2.1B: A HISTORICAL TIMELINE OF HAWKEYE'S EVOLUTION - INTO THE SOPHISTICATED TECHNOLOGY IT IS SEEN AS TODAY.

CAMERA CALIBRATION

START PROCESSING

BALL RECOGNITION

GEOMETRY ALGORITHM

3D POSITION OF BALL

TRACK OF THE BALL

PREDICTED FLIGHT

FIGURE 4.2.1C: *TOP LEVEL VIEW OF THE HAWKEYE SYSTEM - THE PROCESSES THE SYSTEM UNDERGOES TO MAKE AN ACCURATE DECISION.*

Demonstrated in Figure 4.2.1C, HawkEye completes many processes to reach a precise decision – calculating up to one billion equations every rally, in a matter of seconds.

HawkEye has received a mixed reception from players, but has had an overwhelming positive response from fans.
The co-creator, Paul Hawkins, suggested that this was because HawkEye produces immediate results.
"The decision is announced after around a 10 second delay. Coincidentally, this seems to be the optimum time for the crowd to get excited and build the tension. The big-screen visual shows the ball travelling to the line gradually, and the crowd seem to really like this." (Hawkins, P. 2007).

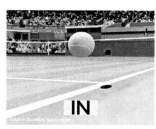

FIGURE 4.2.1D: *A SHOT IS CALLED IN BY HAWKEYE - AFTER AROUND A 10 SECOND WAIT THE CROWD IS EXCITEDLY ANTICIPATING THE RESULT.*

The reaction from tennis players has been mixed. World number 1 Roger Federer describes HawkEye as 'nonsense' and 'inaccurate', independently agreeing with the investigation by Cardiff University (*Chapter 2: Review of Literature*).
However, Australia cricket player, Ricky Ponting, concludes that "the balls moving so fast these days that sometimes it's impossible for anyone to see, even a trained umpire. With instant replay we can eliminate human error."

Rich Kaufman, the United States Tennis Association director of officials, states: "If people saw a player arguing, they assumed the player was right. HawkEye shows officials are a lot more correct than people ever give us credit for."

Not only does Hawkeye aid the umpire, but it also provides a new dimension for viewers at home. World number 7, Andy Roddick, declares: "On top of getting just the calls right, it'll add another aspect for viewers. Two challenges per set will add drama and excitement. This will add to tennis while removing human error."

The introduction of challenges has seen players approaching tennis differently. With an extra challenge in tie-breaks, players use challenges in a tactical way, creating tension between opponents.

Consequently, it seems that HawkEye has established itself in sport as a world leader in decision-making technology.
Some purists do not want this tool, but the majority of players, viewers, and umpires have embraced this technology as a step forward for sport, largely because it makes accurate decisions within seconds, keeping the viewers engrossed, while making the correct decision – it seems like the perfect compromise.

FIGURE 4.2.1E: *GLEN MCGRATH (BOWLER) TO LEFT HANDERS [BATSMAN] - HAWKEYE IS USED AS A VISUAL AID TO EDUCATE TELEVISION VIEWERS AS WELL AS ACTING AS VALUABLE FEEDBACK FOR TEAM ANALYSIS.*

4.2.2. THE UMPIRE DECISION REVIEW SYSTEM

The Umpire Decision Review System is a new technology system being used on an experimental basis in cricket.

The system is being used only in Test Cricket for the sole purpose of reviewing the controversial decisions made by the field umpires.
There are two types of reviews:

1) Umpire Review

The umpire has the option to refer a run out, stumpings, hit wicket, and boundary decisions to the third umpire, before making the final decision.

2) Player Review

A player may request a review of a decision taken by the field umpires only concerning whether the batsman has been dismissed or not.

When referred to the third umpire the following technologies are available:

- Slow-motion replays
- Ultra motion replays
- Stump microphone
- HawkEye
- Hotspot

ONE CRITICISM OF THE REVIEW SYSTEM IS THAT IT SLOWS DOWN THE GAME EVEN FURTHER, LEAVING FANS AND PLAYERS IMPATIENT.

FIGURE 4.2.2A: THE UMPIRE DECISION REVIEW SYSTEM - HAS NOT RECEIVED THE SAME WARM WELCOME AS HAWKEYE HAS EXPERIENCED.

THE THIRD UMPIRE HAS A RANGE OF TECHNOLOGIES AVAILABLE TO ASSIST THE ON-FIELD UMPIRE IN HIS DECISION.

Although the system is trying to link the correct decision with drama and take cricket forward, the reception has been subdued.

"If any single innovation was going to undermine the fragile, ancient contract of respect between players and umpires, it is the review system." (Mitchell, K. 2009)

West Indies batsman, Shivnarine Chanderpaul, is not a fan of the trialled technology: "It's pretty tricky when you are given the responsibility to try and make the decision in a split second. It's quite hard to see the actual line."

WEST INDIES BATSMAN SHIVNARINE CHANDERPAUL ASKS FOR A REVIEW.

FORMER UMPIRE DICKIE BIRD DOES NOT WANT THE REVIEW SYSTEM IN PLACE.

FIGURE 4.2.2B: THE UMPIRE REVIEW SYSTEM HAS RECEIVED A POOR RECEPTION - MAINLY BECAUSE OF THE TIME IT TAKES TO REACH A DECISION.

Former umpire Dickie Bird is also critical of the system because, "they are taking the authority away from the on-field umpires, and the whole thing is causing more problems than it's worth."

There are some supporters of this technology such as the former Pakistan captain Javed Mianda; "With the number of mistakes increasing, I think this review system is good for the game because one bad decision can turn a defeat into a win or vice versa for any team."

However, the overpowering opinion is that the expensive review system is yet to be a success.
It seems that the appeal of sport is that it is

played by human beings, who inevitably make mistakes, which in turn, adds to the theatre and charm. Take that away and you take an essential element that makes sport, especially cricket, enjoyable and educational.

4.3. USE OF HOTSPOT

As identified by Ting and Chilukuri (2009) Hotspot technology is an infrared imaging system used to determine whether the ball strikes the batsman's pad or bat (page 6).

Although researchers such as Mitchell (2009) and Dorries (2009) suggest that third umpires do not trust this tool, and that it "plagues" their mind with "doubt and indecision" Hotspot has been widely accepted into cricket.

Many former players actually state that Hotspot is heavily relied on by the third umpire due to its speedy and accurate nature.

FIGURE 4.3A: HOTSPOT GIVES AN INDICATION AS TO WHERE THE BALL HIT - USING INFRARED CAMERAS THE HEAT CREATED BY THE BALL MAKES A LIGHTER SPOT ON THE IMAGE.

When reviewing these existing technologies there is a clear emerging trend witnessed.
Technologies that produce fast, conclusive, and accurate results are embraced warmly. However, tools that produce slow results, creating crowd distraction, such as the review system, are not acknowledged as moving the game forward.

4.4. USE OF SNICKOMETER

Discussed in *Section 2.1* (page 7), Snickometer is a microphone placed in the stumps, connected to an oscilloscope that measures the sound waves the ball creates.

The response generated from the introduction has been mixed. Some, such as Ting and Chilukuri (2009) argue that the hardest call an umpire has to make is whether the ball has nicked the bat and should be used to aid the third umpire.

Yet, the fact that this tool is not available to the third umpire partly suggests this device is not as accurate as other technologies, and may give the umpire too many tools, that will result in the decision taking even longer to be made.

THE TELEVISION MATCH OFFICIAL TELLS THE PITCH REFEREE HIS DECISION, OR IT IS DISPLAYED ON THE DISPLAY BOARD, WHEN POSSIBLE.

4.5. TELEVISION MATCH OFFICIAL

The Television Match Official (TMO), previously known as the Video Referee, was introduced to rugby union in 1996.

When a try needs clarification, the referee will ask for a review by the TMO. The pitch referee is told either by radio link-up or by the use of a big screen during televised matches of his decision.

USING THE TELEVISION MATCH OFFICIAL RESULTS IN EXTREMELY ACCURATE, BUT FAIRLY SLOW, DECISIONS, IN THE MOST HIGH PROFILE OF GAMES.

FIGURE 4.5A: THE TELEVISION MATCH OFFICIAL.

The announcement of the outcome on the big screen heightens crowd excitement, encouraging debate rather than bringing boredom through delay.

Since its introduction, the reaction has generally been good. Now recognised as part of the game at a higher level, this tool can solve game changing passages of play.
Mark Cueto thought he had gone over for a try in the 2007 Rugby World Cup final against South Africa. However, when taken to the TMO the try was disallowed; Cueto's foot had gone into touch.

The tool has been embraced due to the accurate decisions it reaches. Although sometimes resulting in a lengthy delay, rugby has made the subconscious decision that the reaching the correct decision is more important than keeping the game flowing.

CHAPTER 5: ESTABLISHING THE NEED FOR THE INTRODUCTION OF TECHNOLOGY IN SPORT

5.1. INTRODUCTION

In the 1970s, the Soviet Union's ice hockey coach, Viktor Tikhonov, inspired his team, by insisting that they start every match, by imagining they were 0-3 down.

"A goal for your weaknesses, another for your opponent's strengths and a third for umpiring errors". (Tikhonov, V. 1971).

Scepticism about umpiring errors has not subsided. In the sporting world where stakes are ever increasing and an incorrect line-call can mean a change of fortunes, there is an increasing reliance on technology to ensure that all decisions are unbiased.

Governing bodies are under increasing pressure to use some form of technology to eliminate mistakes that are regularly highlighted by television replays from numerous angles. The reasons for this ever-increasing pressure are discussed below using relevant case studies.

5.2. THIERRY HENRY HANDBALL CASE STUDY

2010 FIFA World Cup qualifier play off – France vs. Republic of Ireland, second leg, 18/11/2009, Stade de France, Paris

FIGURE 5.2A: THE HAND OF GAUL - THIERRY HENRY PALMS THE BALL ACROSS THE BOX FOR TEAM MATE WILLIAM GALLAS TO SCORE THE CRUCIAL GOAL AND PUT FRANCE THROUGH TO THE 2010 WORLD CUP FINALS.

The stakes could not have been higher – a place at the 2010 South Africa World Cup for the winner. Ireland led France 0 – 1 on the night, making the aggregate score 1-1. In the 73rd minute, Thierry Henry handled the ball, passing it across the six-yard box into the path of his teammate William Gallas, who scored the simplest of goals and put France through to the World Cup Finals.

Although television replays immediately showed it was a clear handball the decision could not be changed. The spectacle was overshadowed by the failings of the officials to notice Henry's blatant handball.

On the world's biggest footballing stage, with millions around the world watching, the argument for the use of technology in football exploded in spectacular fashion.

The Irish asked Fédération Internationale de Football Association (FIFA) for a replay, followed by a request for an extra, thirty-third, place in the World Cup to be created – both were rejected, with FIFA pointing to Law 5; "the decisions of the referee regarding facts connected with play are final" as the reason.

Ireland were knocked out in dramatic circumstances.

Irish defender, Richard Dunne, said: "I think it was quite blatant that he cheated. The linesman was in line with the incident, it wasn't a hard decision to make."

Ireland assistant manager, Liam Brady, was scathing of FIFA. "The FIFA president, Sepp Blatter, goes on about fair play – let him reflect on what happened. Where is football going if a team is cheated out of fair play? For the dignity and integrity of football, this needs resolving."

With Henry even admitting it was a handball in interviews moments after the final whistle, a country was cheated out of a World Cup place.
A simple video replay could have shown officials that it was a handball seconds after it happened, yet even at a game with such significance, FIFA refuses to acknowledge this.

"It is clear that mistakes are made, but authorities have an obligation to try and at least appear transparent, and in refusing to embrace video technology, it is a clear breach of duty." (Ingle, S. 2009).

5.3. DAVID NGOG DIVE CASE STUDY

KEITH HACKETT SUGGESTS THAT DIVING IS BECOMING LESS COMMON, BUT STATISTICS SUGGEST OTHERWISE.

IT IS DIFFICULT TO DISTINGUISH BETWEEN A BLATANT DIVE AND A PLAYER WHO HURDLES A CHALLENGE IN ORDER TO AVOID GETTING INJURED.

FIGURE 5.3A: CONNING THE REFEREE IN BLATANT A MANOR – STATISTICALLY, DIVING IS UNFORTUNATELY ONE OF FOOTBALL'S MOST COMMONLY SEEN PROBLEMS.

Premier League match – Liverpool FC vs. Birmingham City FC, 09/11/2009, Anfield, Liverpool

In 2007, Keith Hackett, the Football Association's (FA) head of elite referees, declared that diving for free-kicks was on the verge of being totally eradicated from the Premier League, thanks in large part to the efforts of managers helping get the problem "under control".

However, his assessment is contradicted by officials, who insist diving remains widespread in the Premier League.

Hackett continued: "Yes, of course diving is a controversial issue but it's being handled. Trying to con the referee is deliberate cheating and that has no part in football here."

However, Hackett also states that diving is the most difficult aspect of football for referees to manage.
"We don't have the benefit of replays and instead only have one chance to judge if a player has received sufficient contact to have fallen. So we will get it wrong sometimes and players will continue to get away with diving." (Hackett, K. 2007).

David Ngog recently got away with a patent dive, conning the referee into giving Liverpool a penalty (Figure 5.3B). Steven Gerrard converted the penalty to salvage a draw for Liverpool, denying Birmingham a famous win.
In a Premiership season that has been the closest since its creation in 1992, Liverpool's point could prove vital at the end of the season.

LIVERPOOL'S DAVID NGOG (24) HURDLES THE CHALLENGE OF
BIRMINGHAM'S LEE CARSLEY (BOTTOM).

NGOG DIVES RESULTING IN THE REFEREE GIVING A PENALTY,
AFTER INSTANT REPLAYS VERY CLEARLY SHOW THAT THERE WAS
NO CONTACT FROM CARSLEY.

FIGURE 5.3B: DAVID NGOG'S ACT OF CHEATING AGAINST BIRMINGHAM.

At the time of writing, Liverpool are sixth in the league. The undeserved point against Birmingham may be pivotal in ensuring Liverpool get into the Europa League, earning millions, while Aston Villa, could just miss out at the end of the 09/10 season.

Competition	Position	Team	Played	Won	Drawn	Lost	For	Against	G/D	Points
Champions League	1	Chelsea	33	23	5	5	84	30	54	74
	2	Manchester United	33	23	3	7	77	27	50	72
	3	Arsenal	33	22	5	6	75	34	41	71
	4	Manchester City	32	16	11	5	64	40	24	59
Europa League	5	Tottenham Hotspur	32	17	7	8	58	32	26	58
	6	Liverpool	33	16	7	10	54	33	21	55
	7	Aston Villa	32	14	12	6	44	32	12	54
	8	Everton	33	13	11	9	52	44	8	50
	9	Birmingham	33	12	10	11	34	38	-4	46
	10	Stoke City	32	10	12	10	32	35	-3	42

TABLE 5.3C: PREMIER LEAGUE TABLE AFTER THE EASTER WEEKEND FIXTURES - (HOW THE TABLE LOOKED ON 05/04/2010).

On review, of 18 yellow cards given out in the 09/10 season for diving, only half of these were actually dives; the rest fouls. (Opta Sports, 2010)
As Hackett admits, referees do get it wrong, but this is understandable – having to make a judgement in a split second will always produce inconclusive decisions.

Using video technology, the referee could have decisive help determining if a player dived or was actually fouled. With one point separating teams and consequently millions of pounds of earnings it must be time to help the officials get the important calls correct.

Interestingly, Table 5.3D shows how the 2006/07 Premier League would have finished had decisions been correct i.e. penalties given accurately etc.

- Ninety-seven wrong decisions affected the score-line of games.

- There should have been 20 additional home goals scored and 37 extra away goals.

Correct Result	Actual Result	Team	Played	Won	Drawn	Lost	For	Against	G/D	Points
1	1	Manchester United	38	25	8	5	84	34	50	83
2	2	Chelsea	38	23	8	7	62	27	35	77
3	4	Arsenal	38	20	13	5	71	37	34	73
4	3	Liverpool	38	21	9	8	62	27	35	72
5	6	Everton	38	20	8	10	57	37	20	68
6	11	Aston Villa	38	14	14	10	46	40	6	56
7	7	Bolton	38	15	11	12	47	52	-5	56
8	8	Reading	38	16	7	15	57	50	7	55
9	9	Portsmouth	38	14	13	11	47	45	2	55
10	5	Tottenham Hotspur	38	15	8	15	56	56	0	53
11	10	Blackburn	38	14	8	16	51	56	-5	50
12	13	Newcastle	38	12	8	18	38	48	-10	44
13	12	Middlesbrough	38	12	7	19	44	51	-7	43
14	17	Wigan	38	9	13	16	42	59	17	40
15	16	Fulham	38	8	15	15	43	62	-19	39
16	19	Charlton	38	10	8	20	37	62	-25	38
17	14	Manchester City	38	9	10	29	32	51	-19	37
18	18	Sheffield United	38	9	9	20	34	58	-24	36
19	15	West Ham	38	9	7	22	34	63	-29	34
20	20	Watford	38	8	10	20	32	61	-29	34

TABLE 5.3D: PREMIER LEAGUE TABLE 2006/07 · SHOWING THE POSITIONS TEAMS WOULD HAVE FINISHED HAD DECISIONS BEEN 100% ACCURATE.

5.4. THE INTRODUCTION OF TWO EXTRA OFFICIALS IN THE EUROPA LEAGUE

Europa League match –Fulham FC vs. AS Roma, 22/10/2009, Craven Cottage, London

With FIFA's refusal to implement technology, they instead trailed the introduction of two extra officials in the Europa League.

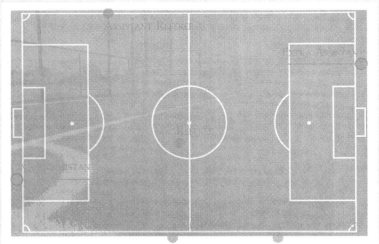

FIGURE 5.4A: THE TWO EXTRA ASSISTANTS - INTRODUCED IN THE EUROPA LEAGUE IN 2009. THEY CAN MOVE ONTO THE PITCH IN A STRAIGHT LINE AS FAR AS THE EDGE OF THE PENALTY AREA. THEY DO NOT HAVE FLAGS BUT WILL BE ABLE TO TALK TO THE REFEREE VIA RADIO.

One of the first European ties to see this experiment in operation was Fulham against Roma in October 2009.   However, Fulham manager, Roy Hodgson, was dismayed that the presence of extra officials did not prevent the referee sending off the wrong player.Everton manager, David Moyes, was also critical of the trial after Louis Saha was dismissed for raising his hands to an AEK Athens player in September 2009: "It's amazing that not one of the five officials spotted that Saha had been fouled first."

World players' union Fifpro polled the captains of the 48 clubs who competed in the Europa League group stages. Of the 31 players who responded, 70% saw no improvement in decision-making during the trial but 90% want to see goal-line technology.

Undoubtedly, the trial with the extra officials has not worked, decisions are still being incorrectly made.   Many managers and players have concluded that this trial has only increased the need for technology in football.

5.5. CHAPTER CONCLUSIONS & SUMMARY OF ARGUMENTS

	Argument	Reasons	Supporting Quotes	Supporting Material
1	Aid officials with difficult calls	Even in vital games the officials can miss crucial, match changing passages of play	"I think it was quite blatant that he cheated. The linesman was in line with the incident, it wasn't even a hard decision to make." (Dunne, R. 2009)	Thierry Henry Handball (Section 5.2) Figure 5.2A
2	Protect officials from abuse by players and fans	With the protection for referees, more people will be willing to do the job, which will result in the standards being raised	—	—
3	Make sport as accurate and fair as possible	Decisions made correctly 100% of the time results in a fairer sport, with accurate scores, winners etc	"Where is football going if a team is cheated out of fair play? For the dignity and integrity of football, this needs resolving." (Brady, L. 2009)	—
4	Eradicate Diving	Diving is cheating within football to con the referee into giving advantageous decisions	"We don't have the benefit of replays and instead only have one chance to judge if a player has received sufficient contact to have fallen over and do get it wrong from time to time and players." (Hackett, K. 2007)	David Ngog (Section 5.3) Figure 5.3B
5	Finish with an accurate table at the end of the season	Table 4.3D shows where teams would have finished had decisions been 100% correct - the difference between millions of pounds	—	Table 3.3D
6	Make officials aware of incidents they have not seen	To create the most fair environment to play matches in as possible	"They have decided to trial this method but it clearly hasn't worked because cameras could have picked up the correct player to send off - unfortunately for us, the referee did not." (Hodgson, R. 2009)	Introduction of Two Extra Officials in the Europa League (Section 5.4) Figure 5.4A

TABLE 5.5A: A SUMMARY OF ARGUMENTS THAT STATE WHY TECHNOLOGY SHOULD BE INTRODUCED TO SPORT.

Football traditionalists will say the referees' decision is always final, but the history of football rules follow the same pattern – exploitation by players, followed by correction from the authorities.

In 1891 for instance, there was no referee or free kicks because it was assumed that no gentleman would intentionally foul.
Regulations such as the offside rule have come about because players try to take unfair advantages.
Introducing technology would eliminate any potential loopholes being exploited by players.

However, the International Football Association Board (IFAB) issued a statement on the 6th March 2010 stating they would not pursue goal line technology.

"The current systems [on offer], with all respect to the companies [who have developed them], are complicated and not 100 percent accurate," (Blatter, J. S. 2010). Yet, this can be counteracted by arguing that the referee is far from 100 percent accurate –technology will always produce more definite judgments than the referee.

The news brought a sharp reaction from Arsenal manager Arsene Wenger, who said it was "beyond comprehension" that global football chiefs had maintained their opposition to goal-line technology.
"For me, it is difficult to understand, because you want as much justice as possible." Wenger added.

"They [FIFA] argue that technology would disrupt the flow of the game. But with players arguing with the referee, we are always seeing the game interrupted." (Ferguson, A. 2009).
Ferguson goes on to say that by protecting referees, their job becomes easier and more people will be willing to do the job, resulting in the standards being raised.

The case studies have demonstrated a clear need for technology in sport. Systems that have been trialled have not obtained players' backing.

The Independent's James Lawton summaries this argument: "As long as FIFA goes on ignoring the need for technology we can be certain of only one thing. It is that the ludicrousness of its policy will continue to be exposed by the consequences of refusing to face a whole list of realities."

CHAPTER 6: ESTABLISHING THE NEED FOR NOT INTRODUCING TECHNOLOGY IN SPORT

6.1. INTRODUCTION

When the IFAB issued their statement, stating that they would not be trialling goal line technology, a highly opinionated argument ensued.

Premier League managers have publically criticised the governing bodies for not implementing technology to make the game more accurate and fair.

Yet, others argue that technology should not be introduced, such as Jonathan Ford, the chief executive of the Welsh Football Association.
"The human element of the game is a critical component of it. It's the thing ultimately we end up debating. That's the beauty of the game and it's what keeps people talking in the pubs afterwards. A stop-start situation where you review all decisions would be the result, and I don't see that as part of the game." (Ford, J. 2009).

The reasons for people's hesitations concerning the pioneering of technology in sport are discussed in this chapter, using relevant case studies.

6.2. FIFA'S POINT OF VIEW

In a statement issued by FIFA, the board indicated it would continue to favour the "human side," preserving the game and not favouring the use of gadgets or delaying for replays.

FIFA PRESIDENT JOSEPH SEPP BLATTER.   UEFA PRESIDENT MICHEL PLATINI.

FIGURE 6.2A: AGAINST CHANGING WITH THE TIMES - HE HIGHEST OF FOOTBALL'S GOVERNING BODIES OPPOSE THE USE OF TECHNOLOGY.

After analysing the thoughts of the most powerful chiefs in football about the decision to dismiss the use of goal line technology, a clear divide was seen.

The majority of players and managers seem to desperately want the introduction of technology but the governing bodies will not entertain this concept.
"The big moments in this sport – whatever they are – get supporters talking and go down in history. That's what makes this sport so vibrant." (Nelson, P. 2009).

FIGURE 6.2B: GRASSROOTS FOOTBALL - BLATTER ARGUES THAT THE INTRODUCTION OF TECHNOLOGY WILL NEED TO BE IMPLEMENTED ALL THE WAY THROUGH FOOTBALL'S HIERARCHY.

FIFA wants to avoid unnecessary stoppages that interrupt the flow of the game and detract from the sport. Goal-line reviews extend into all areas of the pitch and every call in the game.

FIFA general secretary, Jerome Valcke, stated: "If you start with the goal-line, then any part of the pitch will be a potential space where you will use a video. The human element of the game is a critical component of it because it's the thing we end up debating."

Blatter also stated that if FIFA introduces technology at the highest level, it needs to be executed all the way down the footballing hierarchy, or it is effectively a different game that is being played.

Although rugby has incorporated video technology only at the highest level, Blatter also cites the disruption to the flow of the game as the problem regarding football. "In comparison rugby is a slow game – starting and stopping for scrums etc. But we want to keep football that intense, quick game we all love." (Blatter, J. S. 2010).

6.3. HAWKEYE'S TOLERANCE

Inevitably, after HawkEye's impressive claims, many tests were performed regarding the accuracy of the tool.

Collins and Evans (2008) carried out one of the more in depth studies (page 5) and came to the conclusion that HawkEye should remain an interesting tool for the audience but not used to decide important calls.

FIGURE 6.3A: HAWKEYE'S ACCURACY HAS COME UNDER FIRE IN RECENT MONTHS - MANY STUDIES HAVE BEEN CARRIED OUT TO SEE WHETHER HAWKEYE INNOVATION'S ACCURACY CLAIMS ARE TRUE.

"If HawkEye isn't going to provide 100% accuracy, we might as well leave the human aspect in sport and let the instinctive nature of the officials decide upon calls". (Evans, R. 2008).

This is an argument with which FIFA president, Sepp Blatter, agrees, stating that HawkEye has a tolerance of 5mm, and is therefore not precise enough to seize decision-making control from the officials.

"If it was exact then yes, we may consider it, but it's not. Therefore why replace human intellect with un-precise computers?" (Blatter, J. S. 2009).

(See *Appendices* for HawkEye Innovations response).

6.4. THE 'JOHN MCENROE FACTOR'

John McEnroe always had crowds eagerly watching, both for his shot-making, but often to await his on-court outbursts.

The infamous shout of 'you can *not* be serious!' still reverberates around Wimbledon as McEnroe berated the umpire for calling a shot out in the 1981 Championships.

FIGURE 6.4A: YOU CAN NOT BE SERIOUS - CROWDS FLOCKED TO SEE MCENROE'S TALENT BUT ALSO HIS TEMPERAMENT.

Current world number 7 Andy Roddick recalls watching McEnroe as a child.
"I would often watch just to see his court presence, it was always fun watching John."

Perhaps it was because of the sharp contrast to the calm and composed rival, Björn Borg that people loved to watch his personality unfold on-court.

Billie Jean King, a former woman's world number one, recalls how watching McEnroe dispute line calls increased the intensity of matches – making the crowd more vocal. "There is a line, and sometimes he crossed it, but more often than not his outbursts got the crowd involved and intensified the atmosphere – he was great for the game." (King, B. J. 2002).

Many argue that the introduction of defining technology will take away the opportunity for players like McEnroe to express themselves on court.
McEnroe himself stated that: "People want to see personality; they want to see somebody laying it out on the line and caring and I'm not sure that could be done if a concluding system was in place."

6.5. CHAPTER CONCLUSIONS & SUMMARY OF ARGUMENTS

There are many arguments against the introduction of technology in sport.

Blatter has explained that FIFA's goal is to improve the quality of refereeing, making referees more professional and better prepared.

"No matter which technology is applied, a decision will have to be taken by a human. Even after a slow-motion replay, ten different experts will have ten different opinions on what the decision should have been." (Platini, M. 2010).

Many argue that the simplicity of many sports is one of the reasons for their success. People play the same game all over the world.

"This means that the game must be played in the same way no matter where you are in the world. If you are coaching a group of teenagers in any small town around the world, they will be playing with the same rules as the professional players they see on TV." (Platini, M. 2010).

There have been numerous calls from various entities, including commercial, to introduce technology that could help referees. However, Blatter concludes that apart from the major costs of experimenting and testing of technology, FIFA not prepared to take away the responsibility from officials.

However, it seems that the most relevant factor on this side of the argument is that fans love to debate any given incident in a game. Its part of the human nature of sport – and that is why technology should not be introduced.

	Argument	Reasons	Supporting Quotes	Supporting Material
1	Keep the human aspect of sport involved	No technology is 100% accurate, and therefore is not more decisive or accurate than human input	"The human element of the game is a critical component of it. It's the thing ultimately we end up debating. That's the beauty of the game." (Ford, J. 2009)	FIFA's Point of View (Section 6.2) Figure 6.2A
2	Reviewing decisions with technology will disrupt the flow of the games	Stopping to review each decision will break up flowing sport - one of the most loved factors in football today	In comparison rugby is a slow game - starting and stopping for scrums etc. But we want to keep football that intense, quick game we all love." (Blatter, J. S. 2010)	—
3	If technology is used to decide upon important calls, people will want it to determine less vital decisions	People will always want to go one step further - if technology can be used to determine vital decisions, people will also want it to decide upon throw ins etc, which isn't viable due to time constraints etc	"If you start with goal-line, then any part of the pitch will be a potential space where you will use a video." (Valcke, J. 2009).	Section 6.2
4	If technology is introduced at the highest level, it needs to be introduced throughout the football ladder, regardless of the standard	Because the higher level will get the benefit of video replays and lower leagues will not, it will ultimately be a different game that is being played	—	Figure 6.2B
5	Technology is not as accurate as people may think	After numerous studies on potential technologies, it has been discovered that some are not as accurate as they say and that tolerances are fairly large	"If it was exact then yes, we may consider it, but it's not. Therefore why replace human intellect with un-precise computers?" (Blatter, J. S. 2009).	HawkEye's Tolerance (Section 6.3) Figure 6.3A
6	Letting technology have the final say will limit the crowd participation	With players not allowed to argue with the 'correct' decision made by technology, personalities are not as animated or fun for the crowd	"People want to see personality; they want to see somebody laying it out on the line and caring and I'm not sure that could be done if a concluding system was in place." (McEnroe, J. 2009).	The 'John McEnroe Factor' (Section 6.4) Figure 6.4A

TABLE 6.5A: A SUMMARY OF ARGUMENTS THAT STATE THE REASONS WHY TECHNOLOGY SHOULD NOT BE INTRODUCED INTO SPORT.

CHAPTER 7: COMPARING AND CONTRASTING CRICKET, FOOTBALL, & RUGBY

7.1. INTRODUCTION

This chapter analyses the differences between the three sports, establishing the fundamental reasons why some encourage the use of technology and why some do not, from which conclusions can be structured.

These three sports have been selected because they are the most popular amongst the public, as shown in Table 6.1A. They are broadcast regularly, and talked about in the media frequently.

Sport	Competition	Year	Teams Involved	Audience	Source
Cricket	The Ashes	2005	England vs. Australia	7.4m	The Telegraph
	ICC World Cup Final	2007	Australia vs. Sri Lanka	8.6m	BARB
	ICC Twenty-20 Final	2009	Pakistan vs. Sri Lanka	9.1m	The Guardian
Football	UEFA Champions League Final	2009	Manchester United vs. Barcelona	109.2m	Sport Business
	FA Cup Final	2004	Manchester United vs. Millwall	9.3m	BBC Sport
	FIFA World Cup Final	2006	Italy vs. France	715.1m	FIFA
Rugby	World Cup Final	2007	England vs. South Africa	15.2m	Sport Business
	Heineken Cup Final	1997	Brive vs. Leicester	35.3m	BARB

TABLE 7.1A: MAJOR COMPETITION VIEWING FIGURES - FURTHER EVIDENCE AS TO WHY THESE THREE SPORTS WERE SELECTED TO COMPARE & CONTRAST.

Each sport is at different stages regarding the use of technology (discussed in Section 7.2) within the sport. This makes drawing comparisons more effective and relevant.

7.2. THE RESPECTIVE OPINIONS OF THE GOVERNING BODIES

The views of the governing bodies seem to contrast greatly with the majority of fans, officials, and players' opinions.
Discussed in *Section 6.2*, FIFA are opposed to the introduction of technology in sport because they argue:

- It is too expensive to implement.

- Technology will disrupt the flow of the game when decisions are being checked.

- If it is introduced at the top level of the game, it will have to be brought in at all levels so it is same game being played.

However, in January 2010 Sepp Blatter stated: "I'm not absolutely against it. If the technology is ready to adopt, then I am in agreement. If the security of the system is guaranteed then we will introduce it."

SOURCE: TOTALFOOTBALL

FIGURE 7.2A: FÉDÉRATION INTERNATIONALE DE FOOTBALL ASSOCIATION (FIFA) - SEEM TO HAVE DIFFERENT OPINIONS TO FANS AND OFFICIALS.

But the subject was taken to the International Football Association Board in March, it was decided that the idea of technology would not be pursued.

It seems that FIFA remain undecided on the use of technology in football.
Blatter appears to contradict himself whenever questioned about technology – in agreement with the introduction one moment, and then disregarding it the next.

However, the English FA have already stated in the past that they would not be against the introduction of technology.

ENGLAND
RUGBY

Source: RFU

FIGURE 7.2B: THE RUGBY FOOTBALL UNION - HAS ACCOMMODATED TECHNOLOGY WITHIN THE GAME SMOOTHLY.

Fans, managers, and players are vocal in their desire to see technology within sport, and criticise FIFA for ignoring such a potential improvement.
Discussed in chapters five and six, managers have stated their wish for technology.
"I'm surprised that more fans have not abandoned the world's most popular game after so many diabolical decisions determining results." (Gillings, L. 2007).

Rugby has seen the introduction of video replay flourish and become an integral part of the game.

Rugby Union is a slower paced game than football – stoppages for scrums, penalties, and line outs; there are a lot of breaks in play.
This style of play benefits the use of technology as fans are already used to the stop-start feel.

Rugby also implements Experimental Laws. The governing bodies will introduce a law for a season to see if it works, trialling it. Rugby takes an experimental approach, and therefore favours the introduction of technology.

Rugby dispels FIFA's worries that technology needs to be implemented at all levels – rugby already have different rules in place at different levels; for example, juniors play non-contact, touch rugby.
This difference may mean the use of technology at only certain levels is not as problematic as it could be in football.

However, if technology was introduced to football, the stop-start nature will inevitably frustrate fans, because they would not be used to this in a sport that prides itself on the unique quick pace.

The RFU have backed technology within rugby ever since it was first implemented.
The rugby governing bodies are very flexible when it comes to analysing technologies, and always willing to look into newly developed tools that have the potential to make the game fairer and more accurate.
This approach greatly contrasts to FIFA, who seem to be completely adverse when it comes to looking into technologies.
FIFA will not even trial technologies such as HawkEye, which is not only inflexible, but is more than likely to be damaging the game in the long term.

Cricket is the most technological advanced sport of the three.
The ECB have stated their desire to have any technology implemented that will help develop the game.

However, it must also be noted that the crowd present at cricket is in a different mindset to fans that go and watch football or rugby.

Cricket fans go for the social aspect, for a good day out, as well as watching quality cricket. They do not mind many minutes wait as a decision is checked with the third umpire, particularly because a Test Match lasts all day.

The ECB actively encourages any new technologies, and fans support the governing bodies.
Cricket is united in wanting the most accurate decisions, which cannot be said for football. FIFA want to keep the human aspect of the game, regardless that this brings mistakes.

Source: ECB

FIGURE 7.2c: THE ENGLAND CRICKET BOARD - WELCOMES THE INTRODUCTION OF ANY BENEFICIAL TECHNOLOGY, WHICH IS WIDELY ACCEPTED AMONGST THE WATCHING CROWD AND FANS.

7.3. CONCLUSIONS

After comparing and contrasting these three sports, it has become obvious why some encourage the use of technology and others do not.
There is a clear correlation between the speed the sport is played at and potential to introduce technology:

- Football's governing body opposes the introduction most, because it is the quickest paced sport – the referral to video technology could potentially leave fans feeling impatient.

- Rugby already has technology in place, and is widely received as beneficial because there are already many breaks in play – the pauses to check decisions fall into the nature of the game.

- Cricket is by far the slowest paced sport, so the continuing verifying by technology falls effortlessly into the games' temperament.

CHAPTER 8: RESULTS & DISCUSSION

8.1. INTRODUCTION

Interviews were performed (full interviews in the appendices), which conveyed a wealth of relevant information that could not be established with other methods.

This chapter can be seen as an extension of chapter seven – the three sports will be compared and contrasted in greater depth using the professional's opinions as evidence.

8.2. DISCUSSION OF THE RESULTS

8.2.1. THE INTRODUCTION OF TECHNOLOGY

The striking similarity between all three sports is that the governing bodies support the introduction and use of technology.
Although FIFA are opposed to technology, the English FA have backed proposals to introduce it.
"Keeping it out of the game is only harming and tainting the governing bodies' images and doing a disservice to the game." (Walsh, C. 2010).
Walsh goes on to point out that, the referee needs protection from players repeatedly surrounding him after a decision – technology can solve this as players cannot then argue.

Although cricket has many technologies employed already, the ECB share a similar view and backs the use of technology in cricket.
"Anything to help modernise the game is a beneficial concept." (Bourne, M. 2010).
However, Bourne maintains that technology needs to be fair, equal, and promote integrity within the game.

The RFU are delighted with the success of the video replay system, citing this as the reason why respect levels between referee and player are admirable.
"The RFU will always encourage concepts to take the game forward, to gain more fans, but most importantly, to make the game more fair and accurate."
So then, it seems that all the representatives would like to see technology introduced (if it has not been already), but it must encourage a fair and accurate game.

The interviewees were questioned whether the introduction of technology would eliminate officials' mistakes, which is often seen as the nature of the game.

Bourne suggested that umpire mistakes should now be eradicated, due to supporting technologies.
"Stakes are too high to just go with the umpire in the middle – they should be checked 100% of the time when unsure." (Bourne, M. 2010).
Therefore, Bourne is implying that umpire mistakes being seen as part of the game should be a thing of the past – cricket must update and embrace these new technologies.

Walsh cites a comparable point, arguing that referees need protection, and need help with difficult decisions to minimise the amount of mistakes.

"Although Blatter argues he wants the human element in football, players and managers are disrespecting referees more frequently. If referees have the help of technology this disrespect will not be seen." (Walsh, C. 2010).

Rugby however, already has a good composition of human input and technology. The technology aids the referee, and the majority of time a rugby game goes by without an incorrect decision. This is turn results in the players respecting the officials much more.

Blatter believes that should technology be introduced at the highest level of football, it must be introduced that throughout the footballing hierarchy – this will prove expensive and unsuccessful.
However, the set up in rugby proves this can work:
"It is accepted that the video technology is expensive to set up, and is not feasible to implement for lower league rugby games.
However, all games have the same rules, same amount of players, a referee etc; it is the same game regardless.
Although grassroots do not have this tool, it is still competitive rugby with the same goals and objectives." (RFU Representative. 2010).

The introduction of technology has seen sport as a spectacle raise interest.
However, it seems that this was merely a coincidental sub-factor, and never the main aim of technology.
"I think that to anyone involved in football the correct decision will always be more important [then producing an entertaining game]." (Walsh, C. 2010).

Clearly, it appears that the representatives agree that technology needs to be implemented. As long as it promotes a fair and accurate game, it will be welcomed because it eases the pressure on referees and umpires, in turn encouraging respect between players and officials.

8.2.2. THE LEVEL OF INTRODUCTION

The representatives from each governing body independently agreed that technology should only be used for the vital, potentially match changing decisions.
The ECB's Michael Bourne suggested that there needs to be a balance between technology and the reliance on umpires.

Should this balance be achieved in football, FIFA may warm to the idea of introducing technology, while keeping elements of the human factor.

This is a concept already implemented in rugby union.

The RFU representative stated: "At present we have a good mix between technology and human input from the officials."

The FA concur, reasoning that the game's flow will be disrupted should every single call be checked by technology, leaving fans impatient.

Bourne suggests that being able to question every call can promote poor sportsmanship, as players will challenge decisions even when they know they are wrong –just to keep the opposing team waiting.

Introducing technology for just the major decisions, like rugby, has beneficial consequences.
Supporting the referee, technology will assist in getting the verdict correct –pleasing players and managers alike.

The human's [officials] instinct and intuition, combined with clear-cut replay systems, [technology] will provide a positive mix, and have a positive affect on sport.

8.3. PROBLEMS WITH CURRENT RESEARCH

Interviewing three specialist professionals' gives credible research, but only covers a small area of knowledge and viewpoint.

Consulting only individuals from governing bodies may provide in depth answers, but may subconsciously provide distorted responses to show the governing body in a positive light.

8.4. SUGGESTIONS FOR FUTURE RESEARCH

Fans have just as much to say on the topic of technology in sport, and provide another, different, viewpoint to the professionals interviewed.
Some fans' will have experienced incorrect decisions first hand, perhaps as their club is eliminated from a competitions unfairly.

Gaining opinions from members of the public in the form of questionnaires would offer answers to how the public perceive sport and their governing bodies.

However, there are many associated problems. Questions raised when organising this include:

- Who should be asked to fill out the questionnaire?
- People who have a sporting background?
- Should it be age limited?
- How many people should be asked to make the result an accurate representation of the whole country?

FIGURE 8.4a: FANS HAVE STRONG OPINIONS REGARDING TECHNOLOGY WITHIN SPORT - ASKING FANS WILL GIVE AN INTERESTING INSIGHT AND NEW ANGLE ON THE TOPIC.

Evidently, this could not be organised with the time frame of this study, but would present a new, interesting, viewpoint nevertheless.

8.5. CONCLUSIONS

The use of technology is sport is such a widely debated issue that a definitive conclusion will never be made.

The minority will argue that an errorless, machine-run game eliminates the excitement that makes sport thrilling as a subject of conversation and debate.
They will argue that no controversy results in a lack of entertainment, and that it breaks up the flow of sporting spectacles.
And yes, as cricket suggests, technology gives many answers, but a plethora of new questions too.
However, the overwhelming majority within sport do want to see technology introduced.

"Governing bodies use delaying tactics, which only prolongs a sports inevitable progress." (Churcher, A. 2009).

For as long as competitive sport remains reliant on results, an influx of technology will be seen as developing companies come up with new tools, leading to a desire for quantifiable success.
With such importance attached to achievement, it is to the detriment of any sport to accept a degree of chance in deciding results.

If the referees' decision is inaccurate it should be questioned, not by players intimidating referees, seen presently, but by double-checking.
Mistakes, which managers criticise post match, are eliminated, controversies removed and the respect for the referee improves as human error is removed, thus helping to subdue crowd trouble, and most importantly find the correct result.

It cannot be certain to what degree technology will be seen in sport. As more controversies surface, governing bodies will try and solve them as they see fit.

But, what can be sure, is that the debate will continue to rage from two very passionate viewpoints.

REFERENCES

JOURNAL ARTICLES

Ting, S. & Chilukuri, M. V. (2009) "Novel Pattern Recognition Technique for an Intelligent Cricket Decision Making System". Technology Conference; pp. 1 –4

Tellis, W. (1997) "Introduction to Case Study". The Qualitative Report; Volume 3. pp. 3 –5. Available from: http://www.nova.edu/ssss/QR/QR3-2/tellis1.html

PEOPLE/INDIVIDUALS

Bourne, M. (2010) National Lead of England Cricket Performance Analysis. Met with: 11th March 2010. National Cricket Performance Centre, Loughborough University.

Fletcher, L. (2010) Specialist Dissertation Librarian. Met with: 21st Jan 2010. Pilkington Library, Loughborough University.

Walsh, C. (2010) Suffolk Football Development Officer. Met with: 29th March 2010. Suffolk FA Headquarters, Stowmarket.

WEBSITE PAGES

Bierley, S. (2007) "McEnroe plea on HawkEye". Available from: http://www.guardian.co.uk/sport/2007/jun/22/tennis.wimbledon4 [Accessed: 8th April 2010]

Bull, A. (2009) "Umpire's word no longer final as teams get ready to try appeal system". Available from: http://www.guardian.co.uk/sport/2009/feb/03/umpire-cricket-england-west-indies [Accessed: 9th Jan 2010]

Collins, H. and Evans, R. (2008) "We can be serious: Researches dispute Hawk-eye's wimbledon line call". [Online]. 12th June 2008. Available from: http://www.physorg.com/news132487387.html [Accessed: 2nd Jan 2010]

Dorries, B. (2009). "Cricket referral system under fire". Available from: http://www.dailytelegraph.com.au/sport/cricket-referral-system-under-fire/story-e6frexni-1225804691167 [Accessed: 20th Jan 2010]

Financial Express. (2008) "New cricket referral system gets the thumbs up". Available from: http://www.financialexpress.com/news/new-cricket-referral-system-gets-a-thumbs-up/258676/ [Accessed: 2nd April 2010]

Gillings, L. (2007) "Instant video replays -the pink elephant in the living room of football" Available from: http://www.sportingo.com/football/a5308_instant-video-replays-pink-elephant [Accessed: 12th April 2010]

Gledinning, M. (2007) "Record audience for England rugby semi-final". Available from: http://www.sportbusiness.com/news/162744/record-audience-for-england-rugby-semi-final [Accessed: 30th March 2010]

Greenberg, S. (2010) "The 1948 London Olympics Gallery". Available from: http://www.bbc.co.uk/history/british/modern/olympics_1948_gallery_05.shtml [Accessed: 25th March 2010]

Holmes. L. (2007). "Technology needed to help referees". Available from: http://soccer.suite101.com/article.cfm/technology_needed_to_help_referees [Accessed: 4th Jan 2010]

Mac, A. (2007) "Technology in cricket". Available from: http://www.cricketweb.net/article.php?CategoryIDAuto=%203&NewsIDAuto=4392 [Accessed: 6th Jan 2010]

Marcus, J. (2010) "Rejection of Technologies Won't End Debate". Available from: http://goal.blogs.nytimes.com/2010/03/08/rejection-of-technologies-wont-end-debate/ [Accessed: 5th April 2010]

McCullagh, K. (2010) "Champions League tops Super Bowl TV audience". Available from: http://www.sportbusiness.com/news/171698/champions-league-tops-super-bowl-tv-audience [Accessed: 30th March 2010]

Mitchell, K. (2009). "In the blink of a HawkEye, cricket has changed forever". Available from: http://www.guardian.co.uk/sport/blog/2009/dec/24/umpire-referral-system-england-south-africa [Accessed: 20[h] Jan 2010]

Nakrani, S. (2008) "Diving is on verge of being eradicated, says referees' chief". Available from: http://www.guardian.co.uk/football/2008/may/06/4 [Accessed: 4th April 2010]

Norish, M. (2009) "The Ashes will never grip us while it remains on Sky". Available from: http://blogs.telegraph.co.uk/sport/mikenorrish/100001363/the-ashes-will-never-grip-us-while-it-remains-on-sky/ [Accessed: 30th March 2010]

Ogden, M. (2009) "Thierry Henry admits to handball that defeated Ireland in World Cup play-off". Available from: http://www.telegraph.co.uk/sport/football/international/republicofireland/6599687/Thierry-Henry-admits-to-handball-that-defeated-Ireland-in-World-Cup-play-off.html [Accessed: 4th April 2010]

Pilhofer, A. (2008). "A replay system that is a hit among players, fans and even officials". Available from:

http://www.nytimes.com/2008/09/08/sports/tennis/08hawkeye.html [Accessed: 19th Jan 2010]

Renshaw, P. (2007). "Technology in sport - cricket referral system". Available from: http://ezinearticles.com/?Technology-in-Sport—Cricket-Referral-System&id=1604185 [Accessed: 15th Jan 2010]

Roughley, G. (2010) "Football rejects use of goalline technology". Available from: http://www.guardian.co.uk/football/2010/mar/06/fifa-rejects-goalline-technology [Accessed: 5th April 2010]

Sewell, M. (2005) "The use of qualitative interviews in evaluation" Available from: http://ag.arizona.edu/sfcs/cyfernet/cyfar/Intervu5.htm [Accessed: 27th Jan 2010]

Sheringham, S. (2009) "Players lukewarm over Europa League extra officials". Available from: http://news.bbc.co.uk/sport1/hi/football/europe/8548341.stm [Accessed: 5th April 2010]

Smith, W. (2005) "Cricket more competitive than football?". Available from: http://www.cricket.mailliw.com/archives/2005/08/29/cricket-more-competitive-than-football/ [Accessed: 30th March 2010]

Staff, C (2009) "Dickie Bird criticises review system". Available from: http://www.cricinfo.com/england/content/story/438444.html?CMP=OTC-RSS [Accessed: 1st April 2010]

Thaindian News. (2008) "Third umpire checks with broadcaster's Snickometer". Available from: http://www.thaindian.com/newsportal/world-news/third-umpire-checks-with-broadcasters-snickometer_10024048.html [Accessed: 13th Jan 2010]

Weaver, P. (2009) "Sarwan unhappy with Umpire Review System Despite Reprieve". Available from: http://www.guardian.co.uk/sport/2009/feb/06/cricket-england-west-indies-referral [Accessed: 1st April 2010]

BIBLIOGRAPHY

BOOKS

Babbie, E. (1990) "Survey research methods", (Ed. 2), London: Wadsworth

Bell, J. (2005) "Doing your research project", (Ed. 4), Maidenhead: Open University Press

Coakley, J. (2007) "Sports in society", (Ed. 9), London: McGraw Hill International

Creswell, J. W. (2009) "Research design", (Ed. 3), London: Sage Publications, Inc.

Davies, M. B. (2007) "Doing a successful research project", Basingstoke: Palgrave Macmillan

Keppel, G. (1991) "Design and analysis: A researcher's handbook", (Ed. 3), Liverpool: Wadsworth

Kirk, J. & Miller, M. L. (1986) "Reliability and validity in qualitative research", pp. 87, London: Sage

Lincoln, Y. S. & Guba, E.G. (2000) "Paradigmatic controversies, contradictions, and emerging confluences. In Y.S. Lincoln & E. G. Guba. "Handbook of qualitative research pp. 133 –188, Manchester: Sage

Miles, M. B. & Huberman, A. M. (1994) "Qualitative data analysis", (Ed. 2), London: Sage

Nykiel, R. (2007) "Marketing research methodologies for hospitality and tourism". pp. 55 –56. [Online]: Haworth Press

Rudestam, K. E. & Newton, R. R. (2007) "Surviving your dissertation", (Ed. 3), London: Sage Publications, Inc.

JOURNAL ARTICLES

Control & Automation. (2007) "One in the eye". Control & Automation; Volume 2. pp. 39 –41. Available from: www.theiet.org/controlJune/July2007

Creswell, J. W. & Miller, D. (2000) "Determining validity in qualitative inquiry", Volume 39, 3, pp. 124 –130

Fischetti, M. (2007) "In or out?" Scientific American; Volume 1. pp. 76 –77

Hibbert, L. (1999) "Decisions you can't Argue With". Professional Engineering; Volume 1. pp. 26 –27

Hopkins, W. G. (2002) "Quantitative research design". Sports Science; Volume 1

Kvale, S. (1996) "Interviews: An introduction to qualitative research interviewing". London: Sage

Subramaniam, L. V. (2008) "Folk technology". IT Magz; Volume 1. pp. 39 –40

PODCASTS

Football Weekly Extra. (2009) "Ireland's World Cup dreams ended by Thierry Henry". Published: 19th Nov 2009. Available from: http://www.guardian.co.uk/football/blog/audio/2009/nov/19/football-weekly-ireland-suffer-henry-heartache [Accessed: 20th Nov 2009]

WEBSITE PAGES

Anning, P. (2009) "Garner labels review system as a 'gimmick'". Available from: http://www.independent.co.uk/sport/cricket/garner-labels-review-system-as-a-gimmick-1837578.html [Accessed: 1st April 2010]

BBC Sport. (2008) "Taekwondo to adopt new technology". [Online]. Published: 25th Aug 2008. Available from: http://news.bbc.co.uk/sport1/hi/olympics/taekwondo/7581031.stm [Accessed: 15th Jan 2010]

BBC Sport. (2009). "Bristol City 1 –0 Crystal Palace match report". Available from: http://news.bbc.co.uk/sport1/hi/football/eng_div_1/8194875.stm [Accessed: 15th Jan 2010]

Bond, D. (2007) "Video referee right to disallow Mark Cueto try". Available from: http://www.telegraph.co.uk/sport/rugbyunion/international/england/2323866/Video-referee-right-to-disallow-Mark-Cueto-try.html [Accessed: 3rd April 2010]

"Broadcasting of Sports Events". Available from: http://en.wikipedia.org/wiki/Broadcasting_of_sports_events [Accessed: 27th Jan 2010]

Churcher, A. (2009) "Football must use video technology". Published: 27th Nov 2009. Available from:

http://soccer.suite101.com/article.cfm/football_must_use_video_technology
[Accessed: 2nd Jan 2010]

Cornwall, P. (2009) "End the controversy". [Online]. Published: 28th Dec 2009.
Available from: http://www.football365.com/story/0,17033,8742_5805993,00.html
[Accessed: 18th Jan 2010]

Gangal, R. & Raje, S. (2009) "The Hawkeye technology". Available from:
http://sangramraje.110mb.com/files/HawkEye-Paper.pdf [Accessed: 20th Jan 2010]

Grotticelli, M. (2009) "Should video be used to referee all sports?" Published: 25th Nov
2009. Available from: http://broadcastengineering.com/news/video-used-to-ref-all-
sports-20091125/ [Accessed: 23rd Jan 2010]

Jacques, S. (2010) "No technology for football". Available from:
http://www.destinyman.com/articles/show_article.aspx?article_id=f63f03e8-b858-
4372-9b58-3b1b0dead2ac [Accessed: 8th April 2010]

Jackson, J. (2009) "FIFA rejects Irish calls for World Cup rematch after Thierry Henry
handball". Available from: http://www.guardian.co.uk/football/2009/nov/19/thierry-
henry-fifa-rematch-ireland-france [Accessed: 4th April 2010]

Newman, P. (2009) "It's decision time! Cricket facing embarrassing U-turn over new
technology". Available from: http://www.dailymail.co.uk/sport/cricket/article-
1228353/Its-decision-time-Cricket-facing-embarrassing-U-turn-new-
technology.html#ixzz0jw2ttuxR [Accessed: 1st April 2010]

Opta Sport. (2010) "Welcome to Opta. We live sport". Available from:
http://www.optasports.com/?utm_source=Google%2BLatitude&utm_medium=cpc&ut
m_term=Opta%2BStats%2BExact [Accessed: 5th April 2010]

Pinto, P. (2010) "Blatter in favour of 'accurate' technology". Available from:
http://www.cnn.com/video/#/video/sports/2010/04/01/pinto.blatter.technology.int
v.cnn?iref=allsearch [Accessed: 5th April 2010]

Press Association. (2010) "Fifa may implement video replay technology, says Sepp
Blatter". Available from: http://www.guardian.co.uk/football/2010/jan/24/video-
replay-technology-sepp-blatter [Accessed: 12th April 2010]

Riach, J. (2009) "French want Irish perspective". Available from:
http://www.skysports.com/story/0,19528,11095_5704593,00.html [Accessed: 4th
April 2010]

Shuttleworth, M. (2008) "Case study research design". Available from:
http://www.experiment-resources.com/case-study-research-design.html [Accessed:
27th Jan 2010]

Warshaw, A. (2008) "Premier League accuse FIFA and UEFA". Available from: http://www.telegraph.co.uk/sport/football/2294598/Premier-League-accuse-Fifa-and-Uefa.html [Accessed: 7th April 2010]

Yahoo Sports. (2010) "Blatter: Goal-line technology was too costly". Available from: http://sports.yahoo.com/soccer/news?slug=ap-blatter-technology [Accessed: 7th April 2010]

HAWKEYE INNOVATIONS RESPONSE LETTER TO FIFA PRESIDENT SEPP BLATTER

Sepp Blatter
President of FIFA
FIFA-Strasse 20
P.O. Box 8044
Zurich
Switzerland

22nd September 2009

Open Letter

Dear Mr Blatter

The issue of goal line technology is widely debated, and as such we feel it is important that all those involved in the debate are able to do so from an informed stand point. As such, this is an open letter.

We write in direct response to the comments you are reported to have made on the FifPro website - http://www.fifpro.org/index.php?mod=one&id=17196 which documents a Q & A session between yourself and leading footballers. Specifically, I refer to your response to John Terry's question re refereeing which is detailed below. This letter is also a follow on from correspondence and a meeting we have had with your FIFA colleagues headed by Mr Garcia-Aranda in May 2009 which made the same points as are detailed below.

It is encouraging that you state publically that you are in favour of goal line technology if the technology meets the IFAB requirements – real time, accurate, reliable, only for goal line decisions and only for use by the officials. However, as you are aware, the reasons you have given as to why Hawk-Eye could not be approved do not accord with the facts. I hope you will permit us, therefore, to put the record straight.

To deal with each of your comments in turn:

- The Hawk-Eye system provided an immediate beep in the referee's earpiece within 0.5 seconds of the ball having crossed the line, and hence there is no need for the game to be stopped at all. Where has your figure of 5 seconds come from?
- The Hawk-Eye system has 6, not 7, cameras looking at the goal mouth and works in all instances even if many of those cameras are obscured. The whole purpose for having so many cameras is to make it robust in these instances, and the tests conducted confirmed that was the case.
- The Hawk-Eye system was demonstrated to the IFAB technical committee at Reading FC whilst Reading was in the Premier League, and our system has never been installed at a 3rd division club.

- Tennis is very much a 3 dimensional sport – since no court is flat, the height at which the ball touches the ground is essential. The football goal plane is actually more straightforward as it is defined as a vertical plane rising up from the back edge of the line. As such, we encourage you to focus your consideration on IF a technology works rather than HOW it works.

From the tests conducted at Reading, the Hawk-Eye system was shown to be a very viable option and provided the correct result in 100% of the tests conducted. Hawk-Eye has suggested more testing in different environments and different stadia to enable the technology to mature and undergo a more thorough examination. It is clear however that the technology fundamentally works and could be available for use within football if further in-stadia testing and development were permitted by IFAB and if there were decisive signals of intent to justify the investment in further testing.

If it is the case that you would like goal line technology to be introduced into football, please can we enquire why testing of any system is currently banned within Premier League (or other professional league) football stadia? How is it possible for any technology provider to give the re-assurances IFAB require unless they are able to test their system in real match conditions? As you may be aware, the English Premier League is very much in favour of the use of goal-line technology. They have partly funded the development of the Hawk-Eye system to date and were very impressed with the testing results at Reading. The EPL would likely support us being able to continue testing at one or several of the clubs currently in the Premier League.

Whatever the individual views on goal line technology, there is no question that the process for evaluating goal line systems to date has been confusing and less scientific than football fans are entitled to expect. From our 1st hand experience in football and tennis, we would like to offer some suggestions which we believe would benefit all parties concerned:

- A group of independent scientists should be appointed to independently evaluate any system which offers itself for testing against the IFAB criteria.
- The scientists work with IFAB to develop a formal test plan which incorporates as appropriate the IFAB criteria. The test plan may need to differ slightly depending on the technical approach of each system. (eg you would do more tests in varying light conditions for a camera based approach, and more RF interference tests for a sensor based approach).
- The scientists provide a report back to the IFAB committee detailing the performance of each system against the test plan.
- This report is made publically available, so everyone has the same information available to them when debating goal line technology.
- Testing is conducted at the financial cost of the technology provider, but this risk can be offset against a commitment from IFAB that any system which passes the testing will be approved and then able to market its technology to leagues and events.
- IFAB talk to the relevant tennis governing bodies about the technology testing process they conducted and the lessons they learnt.

For many people, the arguments against goal line technology are mostly concerned with the moral fabric of the sport and whether the use of technology would be good for the game. You are the football experts, and we fully accept that you are best positioned to make the fundamental decision:

- If you believe that football is better off without goal line technology, then please use this reason when justifying your decision rather than making a scapegoat out of the technology providers and incorrectly damaging their reputation.
- If you believe football would be better off with goal line technology, then please embark on a fully transparent, scientific process so that technology providers are able to deliver a system which meets your requirements.

We very much hope that this letter enables the discussion over goal line technology to be debated from a more informed stand point, and that no further action is required to protect our name or set the record straight. We would very much welcome the opportunity to discuss this with you in more detail, and we look forward to your reply.

Yours sincerely

Dr Paul Hawkins
Managing Director, Hawk-Eye Innovations Ltd

INTERVIEW 1 –WITH ENGLAND CRICKET'S (ECB) HEAD OF PERFORMANCE ANALYSIS, MICHAEL BOURNE

> **CONDUCTED AT 09:00 11/03/2010 AT THE NATIONAL CRICKET PERFORMANCE CENTRE WITH MICHAEL BOURNE (HEAD OF PERFORMANCE ANALYSIS)**

What is the England Cricket Board's position on the referral system?

"The ECB believes that anything to help move the game forward is a beneficial concept. The referral system has been welcomed by the ECB but can be improved sustainably. We have incurred teething problems that I know many other countries feel the same about. The concept is good, but it needs heavily refining to take it from a good idea, into a great tool."

Does the referral system increase the spectacle for the fans?

"The ECB believes that anything to help move the game forward is a beneficial concept. The referral system has been embraced by the ECB because it is another exciting development of cricket. However, as I previously said, it has to be improved substantially before it is widely received as part of the game."

If this technology is available, should it be made available for every key call/close decision to ensure the match result is as accurate as possible?

"Well, I cannot give you the ECB's position on that but my personal opinion is that there needs to be a balance between technology and the use of reliance on umpires. Although cricket is a slow game already, we cannot have it slowed down any more due to players and teams abusing the availability of the replay.

We already have players appealing decisions when they know they are wrong to do so just to keep out in the middle a little longer, trying to disturb the bowler's rhythm for the next batsman. Two referrals an innings can often already promote poor sportsmanship, and there is no place for that in cricket."

Why have technologies such as Snickometer not been made available to the third umpire?

"These technologies are available to the third umpire but it completely depends on the host country that the match is taking place in. This is because of the cost implication –clearly, if we are playing in somewhere like Bangladesh then these technologies will not be available.

You will occasionally find that a third umpire is using Hotspot and Snickometer but that happens very rarely, one; because they are luxury tools –often too expensive for most countries, but also two; because third umpires do not find them the most accurate of tools. "

Personally, would you like to see funding for the introduction for these two technologies to be introduced to the majority of countries you go to?

"Of course we would like the umpire to have access to every piece of software and technology they can but as discussed, it is up to the host country and whether they can afford it or not. I cannot really see anyone but the host country funding the introduction for the extra tools."

Does the ECB promote the use of third umpires or is the umpire's odd mistake part of the game?

"Naturally, we want the correct decision on every single call. However, this is never possible due to the umpire in the middle getting it wrong, or the third umpire not having access to certain technologies that would give a definitive answer.

I think that before these technologies were created it was part of the game –the umpires decision was final as he had nothing to help him out but now with the emergence of all this tech then we should embrace this and get the correct call every time. Stakes are too high to just go with the umpire in the middle –they should be checked 100% of the time when they are unsure."

Recently we have seen cricket change, the introduction of Sir Alan Stanford's millions and the rise of Twenty 20 suggests that cricket is starting to brand toward a different market. Is entertainment for the fans, or the correct decision the most important factor? Does this depend on the game type?

"I would be surprised if anyone moved away from test cricket –for the traditionalists nothing will ever beat a 5-day test match. However, the rise of T20 suggests that times are changing and cricket is more about entertainment than correct calls. Fans want to see six 6's an over, a hat-trick of wickets, or spectacular catches but ultimately a good game is a fair game and that's why I think that the correct decision will always be the most important factor. Fans can be entertained with all the camaraderie of T20 but ultimately we want to see who wins the game."

So in summary, are you in favour of the continuing introduction of technology in cricket? And where would you draw the line i.e. is there a point when technology could dominant the game too much?

"We will always come back to what the game is about but if this can be supporting with emerging technologies then the ECB is all for this.
However, new tech needs to be fair, equal, and promote integrity in the game, unlike some cases of players abusing the referral system. Any tech that adds to the game rather than deduce is welcomed. But we must think about cost implications; can new nations afford it?
With me being a performance analyst any tech that will help me and help the guys at Sky Sports critically analyse certain plays will enhance the spectacle for fans but also help reach the correct decision in the end."

INTERVIEW 2 –WITH SUFFOLK FOOTBALL ASSOCIATIONS' (FA) FOOTBALL DEVELOPMENT OFFICER, CHRISTOPHER WALSH

CONDUCTED AT 11:00 29/03/2010 AT THE SUFFOLK FA HEADQUARTERS, STOWMARKET, SUFFOLK, WITH CHRISTOPHER WALSH (FOOTBALL DEVELOPMENT OFFICER)

What is the FA's position on the goal-line technology; should we see this introduced?

"Obviously I am not the spokesman for the FA, but I think I can speak for the majority here at the Suffolk headquarters when I say that to keep it out the game is only harming and tainting the governing bodies' images and doing a disservice to the game.
I believe that with more and more hinging on games nowadays, money, reputations, points, referees feel under more pressure, which results in wrong decisions. I do not see the logic behind FIFA's decision not to implement technology that will always result in the correct decision being made. In today's environment of players surrounding referees and little respect between player and referee I feel they need the assistance - they could have it, its not as if the technology has not been developed yet."

Like HawkEye has in tennis, do you think goal-line technology could increase the spectacle for the crowd and fans?

"It depends on how quick the decision can be made."
[The interviewer told Christopher that HawkEye could make a decision within seconds]
"If that is true then yes it definitely could. As you have mentioned the crowd get so involved in tennis, all making noise when the ball is dropping onto the line in the HawkEye animation. With HawkEye reach being accurate decisions in seconds I just fail to see how it has not yet been introduced. I can think of many incidents when teams have been cheated out of results, positions, money - Ireland against France is the obvious example. This cannot go on, people are laughing at the fact such a large, powerful, well funded sport has not got with the times."

Do you think that if this technology is available, it should it be made available for every key call/close decision to ensure the match result is as accurate as possible?

"We need to just concentrate on the major decisions first. I know one of FIFA's reasons for not introducing technology so far is that they are concerned the flow of the game will be broken up and I can see this point of view. If we start trying to determine every call –corners, fouls, dives, even throw ins the games will, undeniably, be slowed down, regardless that the decisions only take seconds to come through. Look at it this way –on average a ball is in play for only 22 minutes of a 45 minute half. That is a lot of time that the ball spends out of play –if we have to make a decision for every time it goes out a 45 minute half could end up being an hour or even more."

Why have tools such as goal-line and instant replay not been made available to the officials?

"Ultimately if FIFA do not want them introduced then they won't get introduced, it is as simple as that. If people such as the technologies developers can convince Blatter and Platini that they are quick but very accurate then there may be a chance of seeing them introduced but they seem like they are rather stubborn people.
FIFA argue that the flow of the game will be broken up, introducing it will be too expensive, we need to keep the human factors still in the game, but I counter that with why not introduce it just in the biggest of games –the World Cup final, the Champions League final, the FA Cup final. I am positive that the fans, players, management; everyone involved would rather take 2 minutes out and get the correct decision than play on at one hundred miles an hour and encounter incorrect verdicts."

Does the FA promote the use of technology to aid the officials or is the referee's odd mistake part of the game?

"The FA have previously stated that they would love to see technology to be introduced but FIFA are so opposed to it –its like they are scared of technology. Football has to develop, has to be evolved for the better, and currently this is not happening. There have not been many changes since the rules creation back in the mid 19th century. Of course, at present, it is accepted that the referees

make mistakes – just ask Sir Alex Ferguson or Arsene Wenger for example. Referees are becoming under increasing pressure from managers, who criticise referees for their performances week in week out, and it is about time they got some protection, some help for key decisions.
FIFA have been enforcing the 'Respect' campaign recently, to encourage players to respect the officials but how can they when referees are missing crucial, sometimes obvious calls. It is time to defend officials, to make the game as accurate as possible and make the players believe in the football setup.
Although Blatter argues he wants the human element in football, players and managers are disrespecting referees more frequently. If referees have the help of technology this disrespect will not be seen."

Recently we have seen foreign investment into football clubs, particularly English, with the result of millions to spend on world class players. Most notably is Roman Abramovich's take over of Chelsea in 2003, buying players for millions in search of 'beautiful football'. Is entertainment for the fans (as it seems to Abramovich), or the correct decision the most important factor in the game? What does this depend on?

"I think it depends on who is giving their opinion. If I offered a ticket to any game in the world to a neutral [somebody who appreciates football but does not support any team], the majority would want to see a game involving either Brazil or Barcelona – both quality footballing teams, who play the game in the correct manor. Clearly, to these kinds of people, entertaining, beautiful football is more important.
However, fans will want to see the correct decisions more than beautiful football, mainly because they would rather see their team win a scrappy one nil rather than play good football but lose two nil for example.
Abramovich wants beautiful football, and that is the main reason behind him sacking Jose Mourinho [because Mourinho was winning, but only with tedious one nil wins]. However, if you asked him what is more important after Chelsea got knocked out of the Champions League to Barcelona last season (due to many poor refereeing decisions) and I am positive that he would have wanted the correct decisions.
I think that to anyone involved in football the correct decision will always be more important. If we can get the balance between the two, like tennis has with the HawkEye challenge system, then FIFA may warm to the idea, but currently, they do not look like they will be pursuing the idea."

So in summary, are you in favour of the introduction of technology in football? And where would you draw the line i.e. is there a point when technology could dominant the game too much?

"The FA is in favour of the introduction of technology – although I am not their spokesman they have stated this in the past. Anything to help move the game forward is a beneficial step in making sure football evolves and moves forward – modernising it will in turn bring new fans to the sport.
As I have already mentioned it would overstep the mark if video technology was used to decide on every single less important calls such as throw ins and fouls outside the box.
FIFA have such an old-fashioned attitude by saying that football should remain how it was created. We have seen tennis, cricket, even rugby develop to become better for the fans, yet FIFA refuses football to join these sports and I for one cannot figure out why. There may be slight implications to this introduction, but the positives by far outweigh the repercussions, which are more than likely to resolved over time.
Football needs to change, needs to help the referees as much as possible. It is ridiculous to have this technology available, to tell us the correct decisions seconds after the referee has made the wrong one – it is time to modernise, time for technology."

INTERVIEW 3 –WITH A REPRESENTATIVE FROM THE RUGBY FOOTBALL UNION (RFU)

CONDUCTED AT 15:00 01/04/2010 AT ESSEX'S RFU OFFICE, COLCHESTER, ESSEX

What is the RFU's opinions on the video replay; has it been a success?

"The video replay has slotted into the game of rugby without any problems whatsoever. Since its introduction, it has become an integral part of the game, with players, officials and representatives acknowledging that big game decisions have been reached fairly and accurately with this technology.

You see football players surrounding the referee at the end of games, if decisions have incorrectly gone against them. In rugby, we are united in feeling that decisions are always correct, because if there is any doubt in the on-field referees mind then he will refer the decision to the Television Match Official.

This is part of why you see the impeccable respect levels from players to referees –because they know any call that is questionable will be decided with the benefit of technology.

So in answer to your question I think it has been a great success –it has made the player referee relationship much stronger, for which many people admire our sport."

Like HawkEye has in tennis, do you think video replay technology has increased the spectacle for the crowd and fans?

"Subconsciously I suppose it has, but that was never its main intention, just a positive sub-factor. The video technology's foremost purpose was to aid the on-field referee with decisions that he could not see or was not sure on, that was always, and always will be its main use.

However, we have seen the crowd warm to it, rather enjoying the tension that the wait brings. I think it will never get to the same level tennis has with HawkEye when the fans really want a decision to be challenged, rugby fans can do without the video technology. But once it has been referred you can tell the crowd are nervous, and tension forms around the ground. It is a pretty special atmosphere if you ever experience."

Because it is already in place, do you believe that it should it be made available for every key call/close decision to ensure the match result is as accurate as possible?

"Well I know the RFU have been questioned on this topic before.

They have stated that they are extremely happy with the video technology [when it came under fire for not being as decisive as it could be] but they confirmed it would not be extended to further decisions within the game.

To be honest, there is not much more the video technology could be used for anyway. Possibly for the collapsing of scrums and if feet went into touch, but the referees and touch judges normally pick up on this anyway, without the need for help.

When compared to football, for example, people complain rugby is a fairly slow game, so we feel that the introduction of more stoppages may discourage fans and take the game backwards. At present we have a good mix between technology and human input from the officials."

Video replay is not always definite, as seen in the 2007 World Cup final when officials did not allow Mark Cueto's try, yet the replays were far from conclusive –should other tools try and be developed to aid the officials?

"I suppose you do get some questionable calls even after the use of technology. As you mention, Mark Cueto's try that was not given is the obvious example that springs to mind. That was a very hard call to make, purely because none of the camera angles could absolutely say with 100% that his foot was in touch.

Perhaps another, supporting, technology could be introduced, but what could you have? Cricket tools such as Snickometer and Hotspot are extremely expensive to set up and run, and could not be applied to the game of rugby.

These calls that are tremendously difficult to call only come up once every five hundred calls so it is not a common problem –the problem was magnified because this [Cueto's disallowed try] was witnessed on the largest rugby stage possible.

Of course, there are companies actively trying to develop technologies but the decision is up to the RFU to implement them. As far as I know, there are no innovative technologies in the pipeline. For now, we will have to settle for just video technology, but this is not a problem - it is a reliable tool."

Football's Sepp Blatter argues that video technology should not be introduced at the top level of football because it would be a different game being played to the lower league games that would not benefit from this technology. Would you like to see funding for the introduction video replay to be introduced further down the rugby hierarchy? Or is it just widely accepted that it is only the highest profile of games that have this video replay?

"Not to sound blunt but I think that this is a fairly irrelevant question! Purely because rugby has shown that the current set up works.
I have never heard of situations where Saturday rugby games need a video replay to conclude whether a guy has gone over for a try or not. It is accepted that the video technology is expensive to set up, and it is just not feasible to implement for lower league rugby games.
I do not know if it applies to football but rugby is the same sport, despite video technology being used in some games and not others. All games have the same rules, same amount of players, a referee etc; it is the same game regardless.
I think people accept we are lucky to have technology at the highest level, providing the most accurate decisions possible. Although grassroots do not have this tool, it is still competitive rugby with the same goals and objectives."

Does the RFU promote the use of technology to aid the officials or should rugby follow football and acknowledge that the referee's odd mistake is part of the game?

"Similar to the last answer – rugby has already proved that the current set up works. It is acknowledged that rugby will stop to review decisions at the higher levels simply to support a fair game. People have come to accept this and see it as part of the game. I think they know that getting the correct decisions is vital to the game."

Recently we have seen the surfacing of rugby sevens tournaments (a faster paced, higher scoring game) which has become extremely popular. It seems that the spectacle for the fans is very important – people go to rugby to enjoy the day out. Is the entertainment for the fans, or the correct decision the most important factor? Does this depend on the game type?

"The spectacle for the fans is always important, regardless of the game type. But we have thousands of fans coming to watch Premiership rugby games all year around, all over the country, so they must enjoy the spectacle as the game is being played now.
Rugby sevens will always draw a strong fan base – fans want to see many tries, one hundred yard run ins and brutal tackles, but you will find this in Premiership games too.
From the RFU's point of view, the correct decision will always be the most important factor. At the end of the day we are attracting large crowds but also getting the correct decisions with the use of video replay, so I think we have a great balance as it is already."

So in summary, are you in favour of the continuing introduction of technology in rugby? And where would you draw the line i.e. is there a point when technology could dominant the game too much?

"The RFU will always encourage concepts to take the game forward, to gain more fans, but most importantly, to make the game more fair and accurate.
Video technology has been embraced all over the world at the highest level because it will reach an accurate decision, and it is recognised that this is the most important factor in determining calls. Anything that aids the referee when video technology is inconclusive will be welcomed but if that day never comes rugby will not fall apart. We could go on with just video replays and still have successful, fair games, while still drawing thousands of people to come and watch the games.
As for overstepping the mark, I think if we used video technology for every single call it would get tedious and boring – pulling the game in the wrong direction.
A good mix of video technology for the big decisions, such as tries, will always benefit the game, so for now, I cannot see the use of technology in rugby changing much."

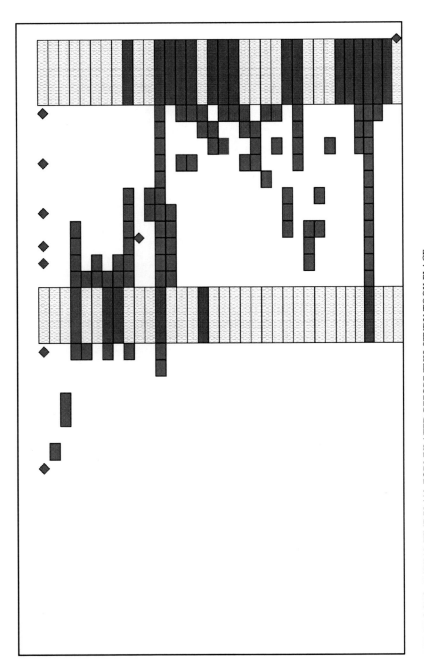

RED BLOCKS - INITIAL TIME PLAN, FORMULATED BEFORE THIS STUDY TOOK PLACE

BLUE OVERLAY - WHEN THE TASKS WERE ACTUALLY CARRIED OUT & COMPLETED

Activity/Week Number	SEMESTER 1																SEMESTER 2								
	1	2	3	4	5	6	7	8	9	10	11	XMAS holiday	12	13	14	15	1	2	3	4	5	6	7	EASTER holiday	8
Dissertation Meetings				◆							◆		◆	◆	◆		◆			◆			◆		◆
Decide on Title																									
Aims, Objectives, Questions Defined					▨																				
Literature Review Research								▨																	
Contact with Library												▨													
Contact Louise Fletcher														▨											
Historical Research																								▨	
Planning Dissertation Structure																						◆			
Analysing Literature																								▨	
Interim Submission									▨																
Summarise Findings																									
Ongoing Compiling of References																									
Research of Existing Technologies																									
Studying Cricket Tools													▨												
Studying Tennis Tools										▨															
Thierry Henry Handball Research																									
David Ngog Dive Research																									
Europa League Officials Research																									
Conclusions to the Chapter																									
Researching FIFA's Opinions																									
Research HawkEye Accuracy																									
Researching the 'John McEnroe Factor'																									
Disruption to the Flow of the Game																									
Conclusions to the Chapter																					▨				
Compare Cricket, Football & Rugby																									
Plan Interview Questions																									
Organise Interview Dates/Times																									
Interview a Representative from the ECB																									
Interview a Representative from the RFU																									
Interview a Representative from the FA																									
Plan Summary/Analysis of Findings																									
Continuation of Writing the Dissertation																								▨	
Conclusions																								▨	
Dissertation Review																								▨	
Final Submission																									◆

RED BLOCKS - INITIAL TIME PLAN, FORMULATED BEFORE THIS STUDY TOOK PLACE

BLUE OVERLAY - WHEN THE TASKS WERE ACTUALLY CARRIED OUT & COMPLETED

Lightning Source UK Ltd.
Milton Keynes UK
UKOW04f2213031013

218466UK00001B/119/P